First Kiss
(Then Tell)

First Kiss
(Then Tell)

edited by Cylin Busby

Deb Caletti · Cecil Castellucci · Roz Chast · Nick Eliopulos
Amy Kim Ganter · Nikki Grimes · Shannon and Dean Hale
Justine Larbalestier · David Levithan · Leslie Margolis
Sarah Mlynowski · Lauren Myracle · Donna Jo Napoli
Alyson Noël · Naomi Shihab Nye · Micol Ostow
Lisa Papademetriou · Paul Ruditis · Jon Scieszka
Robin Wasserman · Scott Westerfeld

BLOOMSBURY

Contents

Introduction Cylin Busby   1

For John Deb Caletti   11

First Last Kiss Micol Ostow   21

The Evolution of the Kiss   **30**

Bad Reputation Cecil Castellucci   33

Yeah, I Know Jon Scieszka   51

How to Avoid a Kiss You Don't Want   **60**

The Third First Kiss Amy Kim Ganter   61

Our First Kiss (with each other)
   Shannon and Dean Hale   71

Breathless Nikki Grimes   81

You Can Take the Girl Out of Texas . . .
   Lisa Papademetriou   87

Improvisation Paul Ruditis   99

Kisses on the Silver Screen   **108**

Read Our Lips
    Leslie Margolis and Sarah Mlynowski   111

Public Service Announcement
    Robin Wasserman   123

My First Kiss(es) Roz Chast   135

Independence, Missouri Naomi Shihab Nye   139

Readers' Poll: First Kisses   **144**

Pashin', or The Worst Kiss Ever
    Justine Larbalestier   145

A Kiss Is Just a Kiss   **160**

Tattooed Love Boys Alyson Noël   163

A Brief History of First Kisses
    David Levithan and Nick Eliopulos   183

Braces Scott Westerfeld   189

So Many First Kisses Donna Jo Napoli   193

The Top Ten Worst Pre-Kiss Foods   **202**

Lips, Tongues, and Dr Pepper
    Lauren Myracle   203

First Kiss
(Then Tell)

Introduction

"He likes you," my friend Missy whispered to me as we sat on the curb, watching our guy friends skateboard down a concrete ramp.

"Really?" I asked, but I had a funny feeling she was probably right. I had caught Mitch looking at me from under his long, dark blond bangs a few too many times for it to be coincidence.

"He asked Bruce if you were going with anyone," Missy went on.

"Uh-huh," I said, trying to act like I didn't care one way or the other. But for the rest of the afternoon, I felt my heart beat faster every time he glanced my way.

A few days later, he walked up to me in the hallway, and, without so much as a hello, asked for my phone number. I scribbled it on a piece of notebook paper, hoping that he didn't notice how my hands were shaking. He called me that night, his voice quiet and low on the phone. "I'm going to kiss you the next time I see you," he whispered just as we hung up. I was so into him, I felt sort of sick to my stomach.

That night, I couldn't sleep. Even though I was almost fifteen, I'd never actually, really kissed a guy before. Would Mitch be able to tell? Where was I going to put my hands? Should I push back his bangs softly and look into his eyes? Where would it happen? In the hallway? Study hall? After school at the skate ramp—with all of our friends watching? After lying awake for hours with smooching anxiety, I got out of bed and flossed and brushed my teeth hard. Then I flossed again. I inspected my lips closely in the mirror, and slathered on layers of Bonne Bell Lip Smacker. I still couldn't sleep, but maybe I was a little bit more ready for my first kiss.

The next morning, when I got to school and saw Mitch in the hallway, I felt a hot blush crawling up my neck, making my cheeks burn scarlet. I went to my locker and waited for him to come up behind me, wrap his arms around me, and make good on his promise. But when I closed my locker and turned, he was gone.

I didn't see him for the rest of the day, and I got back on the bus to go home, my lips still untouched by his. What had changed? Why had he said he was going to kiss me and not done it? Had I done something wrong? Too much lip gloss? What?

The next day, I repeated the whole routine: the flossing, brushing, lip gloss. But another day went by, then another, with no kiss. Mitch called me almost every night, but it slowly dawned on me that the sweet guy I knew over the phone, the one who said he was going to kiss me, was very different from the shy, lanky skater boy I saw at school. And I wondered if the two would ever meet. A quick smile, a glance at the skate park— that wasn't enough for me anymore. I had been promised a kiss; I was ready for one. Suddenly Mitch started to annoy me. Why was he always giving me those weird looks and never doing anything about it? The time for shyness was over. I had clocked a lot of minutes brushing my teeth. I wanted my kiss. I wanted it now.

When Mitch left for spring break, I found myself at the skate park one afternoon with Missy and some of the other girls, watching the guys skate. I missed Mitch, and that glance from under the blond bangs, but it was also sort of a relief to not have to keep up the routine of always looking good, always smelling good, always having clean teeth just in case today was the day. When the guys were done, we rolled over to the pizza place. It was fun just being myself again and hanging with my friends. And as we all walked home, Bruce fell into step beside me, carrying his skateboard under his arm. "Miss your boyfriend?" he asked.

"He's not my boyfriend," I said.

Bruce stopped walking for a second. "Wait, you guys aren't going together?"

"Nope," I told him.

"Well, then I guess it's okay if I do this." And before I knew what was happening, he kissed me. On the mouth. Not too hard, not too soft, just right. I had no lip gloss on! No mascara! I hadn't brushed my teeth since breakfast! And we'd just eaten pizza! How could he want to kiss me now? But it had happened.

And it had been amazing.

I don't remember how Mitch reacted to the news that I had a boyfriend when he got back from Florida, or if he even cared. What lingers is the memory of my actual first kiss, and how different it was from the one I thought I was going to get. You'll see from the stories, drawings, and poems in this book that everyone's first experience with kissing is a little bit like that—not exactly what they expected it to be, but maybe not exactly bad either. Some are messy, some romantic, some memorable, some better off forgotten.

Some kisses are so dreamlike, you're not sure if they even happened, like Donna Jo Napoli's first kiss. Others so dark and mysterious, like Cecil Castellucci's first kiss, that you could spend the rest of your life trying to figure them out. Sometimes your first kiss is so disappointing—like Roz Chast's—that you decide to erase it and replace it with another one, a first "real" kiss. (In the world of kissing, that's absolutely allowed.) And, as Shannon and Dean Hale point out, there are kisses, and then there are Kisses—with a capital K. Only you know which is which, and it might take you a few kisses to figure out the difference between the two.

That's what this book is all about—first kisses. The idea of them, getting them, giving them, erasing them, improving them, (or maybe just imagining them), and the magical way that first kisses keep on happening. When you kiss someone new for the first time, whether you're fifteen, fifty-five, or one hundred and five, you'll still get those butterflies in your stomach, feel your heart beat a little faster. Even if you've been kissing the same person for ages, there's always a new first kiss—the first time you've kissed on a roller coaster. The first time you've kissed in Nebraska. The first time you've kissed as high school graduates, as certified scuba instructors, as newlyweds—if you're creative enough, you can keep those first kisses going forever. And you'll probably want to. Because once you've had that first kiss, whether it's terrible or the most amazing thing ever, you're going to want to keep doing it. Promise.

Deb Caletti

∽∾

For John

This is a story about my *second* kiss.

My second kiss, because this is how my first kiss went: A boy named—wait, I can't tell you his name. Let's call him Randolph, which is actually pretty close. Randolph, who I've known since the sixth grade, calls me and asks me to go to Totem Bowl with him. For a Coke. Sometimes Randolph wears a felt hat with a feather in it, even though all the other boys wear baseball caps. This is true. This is not an embellishment to make the story worse, because it already is worse. I don't like Randolph; besides the felt hat, he is slightly gummy and awkward. Gummy in some hard-to-define way, as if he might spit when he talks, I don't know. Just that you want to keep your hands in your own pockets, out of the way of his hands. And the awkwardness—it's awkward enough that what you think about most is not hurting his feelings. His awkwardness is so large it's almost a third person that you need to be polite to.

So I say yes, to avoid hurting him. I've been taught to be nice. I am the one who helps the retarded boy reach his coat and I am the partner of the girl no one wants to be partners with. It is a bad plan, obviously, this saying yes; I will have to hurt this boy's feelings sometime, unless I want to marry gummy Randolph and die a gummy old age with him just after our silver anniversary. I am postponing the inevitable, and this postponement includes walking to Totem Bowl on a Saturday afternoon. Totem Bowl is a bowling alley not far from our school, with a totem pole out front. The totem pole is right by the 7-Eleven next door. We are fourteen.

I hate bowling. I hated bowling then and I hate bowling now. I suck at bowling. I suck at all sports involving a ball, which means I am good at badminton and swimming. Jogging, if it's not too far.

Inside Totem Bowl, the Native American theme is abruptly dropped. There are cigarette machines and rows of green and red leather shoes worn creepily soft by hundreds of strangers' feet. People in tight T-shirts eat French fries to the smash and clatter of balls hitting pins and pins falling down on glossy wood floors. Drifts of cigarette smoke wind up and disappear. Randolph buys me a Coke and we sit at a table and attempt to awkwardly shove words together, like puzzle pieces from different puzzles. We stir the ice with our straws until the ice disappears, and the words, too. Outside, he kisses me, my first kiss, and it is horrible, really awful, lips shoved together now, and his shirt smells like cigarette smoke making an escape out of bowling alley hell. The kiss is like those olden-day stories where some parent washes a kid's mouth out with soap for swearing, only you want to wash out your own mouth.

It is a kiss, but it is a lesson, too, because we must now fast forward to my second kiss.

Fast forward to: another boy, a second boy, and this time his image comes easily and effortlessly. It is a spring-sweet day and there is the smell of grass and blackberries, and he is just now finished with high school football practice. He has a little swagger, but not an ego-swagger. It's a spring-day swagger, an I-am-so-glad-to-be-here-on-this-day-with-this-girl swagger. He has offered me a ride home in his green pickup truck, and I have accepted. I am smiling so deeply I am sure my bone marrow smiles, too. He takes my fingertips in his, and my fingers have never been so happy. He is a good person. He makes me laugh. He has English homework he needs to do, and he will do it and turn it in mostly on time. He will grow into the kind of man, I am sure, who will mow the lawn and grow carrots in a garden and be gentle with children. He will love his work and know how to make a red sauce for spaghetti and will tell you the names of trees when you go for a walk.

He leans toward me and his lips meet mine and his breath tastes like milk and the kiss is as right as warm sidewalks and plums bought at roadside stands. All of me knows that it's right, every piece of me. This is not about being nice, not a half-hearted offering of myself where I shouldn't offer myself, not about the *idea* of liking someone but of actually liking HIM, really liking him, and it is perfect even if our tongues do that bumbling thing people do in a hallway when they can't quite figure out how to pass one another. We both go this way, we both go that way, and then . . . there.

We get in his truck. The windows are down, and the wind whips my hair in front of my face and I tuck it behind my ear. He has Springsteen in the tape player and he keeps holding my hand even after it gets sweaty. After he stops the truck but before he shuts off the engine, we kiss again, and already we've gotten better. It's so easy. It's like we've kissed a thousand times before, somewhere else.

And what I learned then (something I will forget for too long and remember again only years later) is this: when you don't like Randolph, don't go to Totem Bowl. When you don't like bowling, don't tie on the awful red and green shoes. Offering what should never be offered, (you, yourself) to people who don't deserve it—it brings you bad things. It brings painful awkwardness and cigarette stubs in parking lots and totem poles next to fluorescent-lit convenience stores. Sometimes, a lot worse things.

But a green truck, a spring day, a second chance, means this—when you like a boy, really like him, *love,* a man, too, when he likes you, when his heart is good, a kiss is right. A kiss is amazing. A kiss is warm sidewalks and plums bought at roadside stands. A kiss is the ocean sparkling and a rush of joy like a wave you can ride on . . . maybe for a long, long time.

Deb Caletti is the award-winning author of *The Queen of Everything*; *Honey, Baby, Sweetheart*; *Wild Roses*; and *The Nature of Jade*. In addition to being a National Book Award finalist, Deb has gained other distinguished recognition for her work, including the PNBA Best Book Award, the Washington State Book Award, and School Library Journal's Best Book award, and finalist citations for the California Young Reader Medal and the PEN USA Literary Award. Her books have also been an IRA Notable Book, an SSLI Book Awards Honor Book, and have made the New York Public Library's Best Books for the Teen Age and Chicago Library's Best Books lists, among others. Her fifth book with Simon & Schuster will be *The Fortunes of Indigo Skye*. Paul G. Allen's Vulcan Productions has recently acquired production rights to all five of Deb's novels; working with producer/director Rick Stevenson, Vulcan and Caletti plan to develop the novels into a film series titled *Nine Mile Falls*. Deb grew up in the San Francisco Bay area and now lives with her family near Seattle.

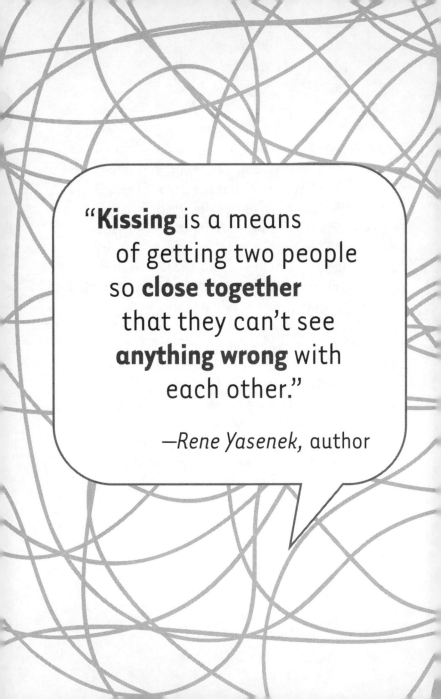

Micol Ostow

❦

First Last Kiss

f, when I was thirteen, and still a kiss-virgin, you had told me that my most lack-luster, most uninspired smooch would also be my most heartbreaking, I would have thought you'd lost your mind.

If you had told me that kiss would be shared with a wannabe surfer boy from Bergen County, New Jersey, I would have laughed hard enough to almost pee my pants.

If you had told younger (thinner, dumber, permed-er) me about the gut-wrenching phe-nomenon known as the "last kiss," I would have shrugged. Would have thought a last kiss *had* to be better than none at all.

When I was thirteen.

When I was sixteen, I met Brandon.

This is what Brandon called me: "phantas-magorical." The only other person, to my knowledge, ever to use that word was Edgar Allan Poe. Brandon appealed to my literary interests; I was a still-pretty-skinny (dance lessons and track team), slightly-less-naive (lame makeout sessions at Boone's-drenched house parties), better-coiffed (via Millburn, New Jersey's finer salons) *book nerd* (still am, really, pretty much).

Brandon was skinny and blond, with hair that flopped over one eye in a style made popular by various teen dramas of the time. His bottom front teeth were slightly crooked and his eyes twinkled somewhere just between blue and green on the color spectrum. Girls liked him; he knew this, and he had his "aw, shucks," demeanor down pat.

Brandon was the first boy to pursue me in the truest sense of the word; I knew not to underestimate the value of a twenty-dollar vocab word dropped by a hottie in brightly colored board shorts, so when pursuit led to the first time a boy shyly took me by the hand and asked—asked!—if he could kiss me, of course I said yes.

Just like in a bad teen drama, the music swelled, if only in my head, and I was aware of nothing beyond his face moving closer to my own. Everything about him from the tips of his eyelashes to the smell of the hair that fell across his forehead was mine to explore. His top teeth ground into my bottom lip while we kissed.

Poe might have called it "phantasmagorical." Or, at least, I did.

So Brandon was the first kiss that curled my toes and sent my eyebrows shooting toward my scalp, and then he became my first boyfriend (thirteen-year-old me would have *totally died*). Which led to a whole other series of firsts: the first time a boy wraps one arm around you protectively and introduces you to his friends as "girlfriend," the first time you spend holidays with a family other than your own, the first time someone sends you a Valentine's Day card that's a little bit sexy, in addition to being sweet.

Sixteen-year-old me was doing pretty well. It could have been endorphins from running track, or chemicals from the salon making me woozy. But it probably wasn't.

It was probably Brandon.

Here's another fun first: the first time he cheats on you (neither thirteen nor sixteen-year-old me ever saw it coming).

I heard from a mutual friend that he'd been out somewhere without me. There'd been beer involved, and then some face-sucking with a girl from another nearby school. When I asked Brandon about it, he didn't deny anything. So once the urge to vomit passed, I broke up with him. My first breakup.

Immediately afterward, this is what I did: I was *angry*. Actively so, though I often kept it to myself.

Sometimes I was angry sitting on my bed and

staring off into space, sometimes I was angry turning circles in dance class, sometimes I was angry not-reading for World History.

Occasionally I moved from my bed to the couch in the den, or sometimes I ate ice cream instead of staring off into space. Sometimes I ranted on the phone to a friend while skipping track practice or tap class. But there wasn't a whole lot of variety in my routine; the biggest change-up was the exhilarating transition from mad to sad.

Which was, I suppose, inevitable.

One afternoon, a thought occurred to me: the very last time that I'd kissed Brandon had been completely perfunctory and lackluster. The weekend before he christened himself a total sleazebag, we'd kissed goodbye after school. It was a quick peck, both of us distracted. No arching eyebrows, no prickly hairs on the back of my neck, no overwhelming sensation of being wrapped up inside of someone else. I didn't think to savor the smaller, almost unconscious moments of affection and intimacy that I'd had with my boyfriend; I took for granted that they'd always be there. That he'd always be there.

Someone must have told me that, or something, back when I was thirteen. Quite misleading.

My last Brandon kiss had been a total washout. Autopilot. But how could I have known? Later, I'd learn that it was always this way with last kisses. Hindsight and all that. But the *first* last kiss? Yeah, that one stays with you. You wish you could—*whoosh!*—zoom back in time and warn yourself (and maybe offer some helpful feedback regarding the permed-hair phase of development).

Hair product is much easier to wash off than heartbreak. It's just a fact that remains true long after you've tossed your tap shoes and traded in your volumizing gel for a straightening iron.

My first last kiss sucked, no doubt. But it was a chance for another first—endless firsts, really—with someone else. And any-age-me kind of likes the promise of possibility.

Especially when there's kissing involved.

Micol Ostow is a veritable virtuoso of romance. She has written three books for the Simon Pulse Romantic Comedy line, and her novel *Students Across the Seven Seas: Westminster Abby* was named a Booklist 2005 Top Ten Romance Books for Youth selection. As a general rule, she does not kiss and tell. But there are ways of making her talk (usually involving chocolate). Visit Micol at www.micolostow.com.

The Evolution
of the Kiss

Although anthropologists still debate over when the act of kissing began, many agree that it is a way for prospective mates to assess each other's pheromones for biological compatibility. Romantic, no? However the kiss began, it soon spread across the world, with many cultures adopting different methods for expressing affection . . .

💜 Ancient Romans kissed sacred items and statues to indicate respect.

💜 Ancient Egyptians never kissed with their mouths, only with their noses.

💜 The Chinese didn't practice the act of kissing until it was introduced to them by Westerners.

- In the sixth century, France was the first to accept kissing in courtship. However, the origin of the term "French kiss" was not from France, but rather from the United States, as a way to stereotype sexuality in French culture as over-the-top.

- In Naples, Italy, in the sixteenth century, kissing was a major offense — punishable by death.

- It is considered taboo to kiss in public in Japan today.

- In Belgium, it is customary to kiss anyone who is more than ten years your senior three times, as a showing of respect.

- The Eskimo kiss, prevalent among the Inuit tribes, is not actually a kiss at all, but rather a means for greeting fellow tribespeople when the temperature is too cold to shake hands.

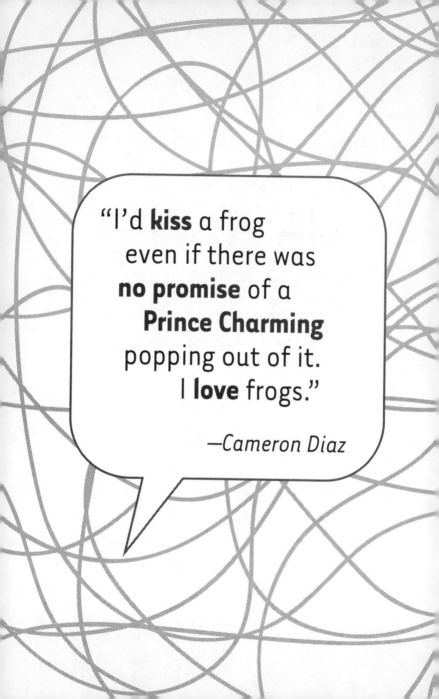

"I'd **kiss** a frog
even if there was
no promise of a
Prince Charming
popping out of it.
I **love** frogs."

—Cameron Diaz

Cecil Castellucci

Bad
Reputation

avid Kahn and I never talked at school. He was too tough. Rumor had it that he carried a switchblade. You'd never think he was the kind of kid who would to look at him. He looked more like Bambi than a bad boy. He wore a faded stone-washed denim jacket, had luscious curly hair and very long eyelashes. But David Kahn had a bad reputation and so did his friends John Little and Kenny Brodkowitz. John Little was, hands down, the meanest kid in school. John Little was so mean that he most often didn't even wear a shirt. He'd walk around bare-chested with his shirt stuffed and hanging out of his back pocket. And he smoked. Kenny Brodkowitz was as large as a truck and looked like a college football player even though we were only in the sixth grade. David was their soft and quiet ringleader. He could charm them out of any trouble they got into with his good looks, popularity, and innocent-looking doe eyes. But everyone in sixth grade knew better. Those boys were trouble with a capital T, and my friends and I knew to stay away from them.

David Kahn and his crew were popular. At least that's what my friends said. And we weren't. At least that's what we knew. We knew we weren't popular because we read books, cried when John Lennon died, went to the library, and liked outer space. We were definitely not cool. We were brains.

So I don't really know how it started. I don't know how I caught David Kahn's eye. I think maybe he lived across the street from me. He must have lived near me because one day, out of the blue, he rang my doorbell and asked me if I wanted to come outside and play.

"Sure," I said. I knew better than to say no to David Kahn.

"Cool," he said.

I put my sweater on and went downstairs. He didn't have a ball or anything and there was no one else with him, so I knew it wasn't like we were going to start a game of kick ball, or play *Charlie's Angels*, or anything like that.

"What do you want to do?" I asked.

"I don't know," he said. "Hang out on the island?"

In the middle of my street there was an island that split the road in two. The island had trees growing on it and a rock big enough for sitting on and I liked to think of it as a secret forest. It was a place to hide out from the world, and if you squinted, the redbrick apartment buildings that surrounded the street would disappear.

That island was a magical place.

We crossed the street and sat on the rock. We didn't talk. I was the kind of girl who always had plenty to say, so I know I wasn't talking because I was nervous. I knew from history class that David

Kahn wasn't much of a talker. He was more the strong, silent type.

He took my hand and held it.

My heart was beating really fast and I noticed that his eyes were really brown. I noticed this because he was looking right back at me. Right in my eyes.

And then he leaned in and kissed me.

It was electric.

We kissed and kissed and kissed until it was time for dinner.

"See ya," he said, not even walking me to my door.

"Yeah," I said, walking on air.

The next day I saw him at assembly and he was standing across the way with Kenny and John.

"Oh my God, David Kahn is looking over here," Jodi said.

"Don't look him in the eyes, he might use his knife," Judith said.

"Ew. Why doesn't John Little ever wear a shirt?" Michelle said.

"Do you think David Kahn really has a knife?" I say.

My friends all nodded their heads. Yes.

A teacher was talking to the boys and then they spit out their gum and John put his shirt back on. The bell rang and we lined up to go into the auditorium.

I don't know if it was me who was ignoring him or if it was him ignoring me. One thing was for sure, we were totally ignoring each other at assembly.

Then we ignored each other at recess. We ignored each other in history class. We ignored each other at lunch. We ignored each other when the bell rang. And we ignored each other after school.

After the obligatory hanging out and going to the pizza place on Johnson Avenue, I said good-bye to my friends and went home to do my homework.

A little while later, the doorbell rang.

"Hey," David said.

"Hey," I said.

"Wanna come outside?" he said.

"Sure," I said.

I knew what we were going to do. We went straight to the island and once we were there, masked from the world by the trees, we sat on the rock and we held hands and kissed.

His lips were so soft and his tongue was nice. I liked his loose curls. I liked the way he rolled up the sleeves of his denim jacket. I liked the way he had a little bit of dirt on him. I liked the way he held me in his arms.

I liked the kissing and kissing and kissing.

I liked the way the kissing made my heart beat faster.

I liked kissing David Kahn, even if his middle name was Trouble.

Soon the sun started going down and it was time for us to go to dinner.

"See you tomorrow," he said.

"Yeah," I said.

I knew what he meant. He meant here, at the rock, kissing me. He didn't mean in fourth period history class. Or at assembly while saying the Pledge of Allegiance. Or in the lunchroom over sloppy joes.

He meant in secret, and after school.

The next day at school, I ignored him all day and he ignored me.

The next day after school, I was kissing him at the rock.

That's how it started and then turned into weeks and weeks of secret kissing.

Weeks and weeks of glancing at each other during recess and history class and assembly. Weeks and weeks of never saying anything, not even hello, at school.

After kissing, I would rest my head on his shoulder.

I wondered where he kept his switchblade and if he even had one. I wondered why Kenny Brodkowitz never spoke a word to anyone. I wondered why John Little never wore a shirt.

I wanted to ask him, but I didn't because David and I didn't really talk. We just kissed.

"I need your address," he said one day.

"Why?" I said.

Maybe, I thought, since we never talked he was going to write me a letter.

"It's my Bar Mitzvah," he said.

I loved Bar Mitzvahs. They were fancy and there was always dancing. I wish I could have had a Bat Mitzvah.

Pretty much everyone from school except my good friends were going to David's Bar Mitzvah.

I wore my Gunne Sax dress and feathered my hair as best as I could.

When the music came on, I was sure that David would dance with me. But he didn't. He danced with every other girl but me.

I danced with his uncle. And his grandfather. And his dad. And they all loved me.

They all said, "Oh, you're a catch!"

But I didn't feel like a catch. I felt like a loser.

They probably danced with me because they felt sorry for me, the only thirteen-year-old not dancing with David at the Bar Mitzvah.

I went to the bathroom.

When I came out, David was standing there.

"Hey," he said.

"Hey," I said.

"There's an empty ballroom right here," he said. "It's totally empty."

"Spooky," I said.

He took my hand and I let him take it because I liked it when he held my hand, and we pushed open the door. The lights in the closed ballroom were dim and there were mirrors everywhere. There was a movable divider separating this ballroom from the one where David's Bar Mitzvah was and we could hear the music from the band spilling into the room.

He kissed me and I don't remember what song was playing. I thought I should try to remember, but my heart was beating too loudly for me to hear. When David Kahn kissed me, I couldn't concentrate.

We kissed for bit and then went back to the party separately.

Monday at school, everyone was talking about David's Bar Mitzvah. Everyone agreed that it was the best one of the year.

"So David's Bar Mitzvah was fun?" Jodi asked me at recess, and I could tell she was trying not to sound jealous.

"It was okay," I said. I didn't want to make her feel bad.

"Weird that you were invited," Judith said.

"We're in history together," I said. They didn't have any classes with David Kahn. I knew this for a fact.

"Are we going to the dance at the teen center on Friday?" Michelle said.

"Sure," I said.

When it was time to go back into school, I saw David still leaning against the wall with Kenny and John. He saw me with my friends. We did not say hello.

Friday night came and Jodi, Judith, Michelle, and I walked over to the junior high school to the teen center dance. The gym was decorated with streamers, there was loud dance music playing, and there was a strobe light.

We all stood against the bleachers, uncertain how to get onto the dance floor without boys.

"Hey."

I knew that voice. It was David Kahn. He had come over to me and my friends with John Little and Kenny Brodkowitz.

"Hey," I said.

"Do you girls want to dance?"

"Uh, okay," we said. Me and my friends knew it was better to dance with boys than to stay on the sidelines all night, even if those boys had a bad reputation.

The boys led us to the dance floor and we danced. I was dancing with David Kahn, and this time I could hear the song. It was "Tainted Love." The strobe light made our faces look scary, but David and I were smiling.

We were so hot after dancing up a storm that

we girls wanted to get some fresh air and the boys followed us outside. John and Kenny tried to chat up Jodi, Judith, and Michelle.

David motioned for me to follow him, and I did. David and I moved behind a tree.

I wondered if he was my boyfriend. I wanted to ask him if I was his girlfriend, but instead we leaned toward each other and kissed.

"What are you doing?"

David and I stopped kissing. David wiped his mouth on his jacket.

Michelle was standing there staring at me with her hand on her hip. She looked angry.

"Kissing?" I said. But I said it like a question.

Jodi and Judith joined Michelle. John and Kenny weren't with them. I think David took this as a bad sign and left.

He didn't say goodbye to me and I didn't say goodbye to him.

"You were kissing David Kahn. David Kahn is trouble. He has a bad reputation. He will give you a bad reputation."

"Yeah," Jodi said. "You could get pregnant the way you were kissing him."

"No, I couldn't," I said. My parents were scientists; I knew how babies were made.

"People might see you kissing David Kahn and think you are a slut," Judith said.

"But I'm not a slut," I said.

I wasn't. Other girls kissed boys at parties. At Seven Minutes in Heaven. At Spin the Bottle. At Post Office. And they weren't sluts.

But maybe this was different. This was *secret* kissing. This was don't-tell-anybody-we're-kissing kissing. This was deliciously dangerous kissing.

"The way you were kissing you looked just like a slut," Michelle said.

"Don't tell anyone," I said.

"Just don't kiss David anymore," Jodi said.

"Or else you'll be a slut," Judith said.

"We don't want to be friends with a slut," Michelle said.

"We don't want a bad reputation," Jodi said.

Judith nodded. She agreed.

I didn't want to be a slut. I didn't want to be a girl with a bad reputation. I didn't want to lose my friends.

I knew what I had to do.

When David rang the bell the next day I didn't open the door. I pretended that I wasn't home. I watched him standing there at the buzzer. I was glad that at least he rang the bell three times before he gave up and walked away.

And me, I cried a little.

Because I never spoke to him at school.

And I missed kissing him like crazy.

Because he was a such a great kisser.

Cecil Castellucci has published four novels for young adults: *Boy Proof*, which was a 2006 American Library Association BBYA and Quick Pick for Reluctant Readers, *The Queen of Cool, Beige,* and the graphic novel *The PLAIN Janes*. In addition to writing books, she writes plays, makes movies, and occasionally rocks out. She lives in Los Angeles, California. For more information go to www.misscecil.com.

"The **first kiss** I had was the **most disgusting** thing in my life. The girl injected about a **pound of saliva** into my mouth, and when I walked away I had to **spit it all out**."

—*Leonardo DiCaprio*

Jon Scieszka

❧

Yeah, I Know

For months I had been desperately hoping to kiss a girl, any girl. But I ended up kissing Patricia McDonald* almost by accident.

As a seventh-grade boy at a Catholic school, I had heard plenty about kissing. All from other boys. Bill Modford, the star of our basketball team, had been telling us for months what a great kisser he was. My older brother, Jim, was

*All names have been mangled by time and memory.

dressing up for dates, definitely kissing. And now even my best friend, Tim Javorsik, was talking kissing.

"Man, it is so great kissing a girl," said Tim.

"Yeah, I know," I said.

"Kathleen Murphy is a great kisser," said Tim.

"Yeah, I know."

"I kissed her over by the slides yesterday," said Tim.

"Yeah . . . What?"

Now the pressure was really on. Even my best friend had kissed a girl. I was in serious danger of becoming the only guy in seventh grade who had never kissed a girl. I had to do something. So I decided to ask my brother Jim for advice. My careful research went something like this:

Me: Man, it sure is great kissing girls, isn't it?

Jim: Is that my good shirt you're wearing?

Me: It's cool how a guy just says something, then the girl kisses him, right?

Jim: Take it off or I am going to pound you.
Me (taking off shirt): Yeah, it sure is great
  kissing girls.

I really wanted to kiss a girl. I knew I had to kiss a girl or become a social reject. But I wasn't really sure that I liked any of the girls in my seventh-grade class. They were all a complete mystery to me.

I lived with five brothers and had no idea what girls were really like. I knew they weren't very good at baseball. They didn't seem very interested in the same comic books or TV shows my friends and I liked. They talked way more than any guys I knew. They laughed at the strangest things. And they couldn't take a friendly punch like even my smallest brother, Jeff, could.

But out of all the girls, when Patricia Mc-Donald, with her short blond hair and braces, smiled at me, something happened. Something outside of my baseball/comic book/all-brother world welled up inside me and started my heart racing. I had no idea what this something was. But I was sure it was meant to lead to kissing.

I tried to find some common ground with Patricia McDonald. But another problem with seventh-grade girls is that they are very hard to approach. They always seem to stand around in protective groups of at least three or four. If you want to talk to one girl, you are going to have to face all of them. So the closest I ever got to talking to Patricia was a wave or a quick "How about that math test?"

Not good.

I was miserable. I just knew I was going to become an old man, or at least an eighth grader, who had never kissed a girl.

Then my pal Tim Javorsik changed my life.

"Man, girls are weird," said Tim.

"Yeah, I know," I said.

"Jane Koontz just told me Patricia might kind of like you and wants to know if you are going to the dance tonight."

"Yeah, girls are—*huh*? What? Patricia? Dance?"

Whatever there was of my seventh-grade brain must have then just blown all its circuits. I have absolutely no memory of all of the things I'm sure must have happened next—like sending Tim back with a message saying I might kind of like Patricia too, getting ready to go to the dance, walking across the gym floor to where all of the girls stood, the song that was playing, actually asking Patricia to dance . . .

Nothing.

Memory returns with my right hand on Patricia McDonald's hip, my left hand holding her right hand. I remember thinking: I didn't know girls were this solid. I didn't know girls were this warm.

I had forgotten all about kissing. I was actually, sort of, dancing with a girl. We shuffled/rocked to the end of the song. I had not a thought in my head. The song ended. We held on to each other. Patricia, with her short blond hair and braces, looked at me and smiled. She closed her eyes.

We kissed.

Her lips were soft and warm. She tasted like

flowers and a little bit of rubber bands. It was like nothing I had ever known. I was dazed, relieved, thrilled, and stunned.

We fell apart, retreated to our rival packs of seventh-grade boys/seventh-grade girls on either side of the school gym.

"Man, you were kissing Patricia McDonald," said Tim.

"Yeah, I know," I said. But this time with feeling.

Jon Scieszka was born in Flint, Michigan, on a Wednesday. Around lunchtime. He is the second oldest, and nicest, of six Scieszka boys. Jon taught elementary school for ten years, raised a daughter and a son, and has written books for kids for the past fifteen years, many with illustrator Lane Smith, including The Time Warp Trio series, *Cowboy & Octopus,* and *The Stinky Cheese Man and Other Fairly Stupid Tales*. He is also the author of the preschool publishing program called Trucktown. Jon is the founder of GUYS READ, a program designed to inspire more boys to read. He lives in Brooklyn, New York, with his wife.

How to Avoid
a Kiss You Don't Want

◆ Don't make eye contact and just keep your head down—there's less access to your lips.

◆ Turn your head so the kisser gets your cheek instead.

◆ Say you're taken. This one works only if 1) it's true, or 2) you're sure you'll never see the person again.

◆ Head to the bathroom—it's the one place where someone is definitely not going to follow you.

◆ Keep friends by you at all times. That way you will always have someone watching your back.

◆ Keep talking. There won't be silence long enough for the person to make a move.

◆ Wear a retainer.

Amy Kim
Ganter

The Third
First Kiss

Based on actual events...

THE THIRD FIRST KISS
By Amy Kim Ganter

Ever since I was little, I'd daydream about my first kiss.

SIGH

I'd imagine it to be the most awesome, life-changing thing ever. It'd be the best feeling in the world!

After all, that's what movies told me.

But my first kiss wasn't so great. In fact, it was quite gross.

(college boyfriend) →

All I could think about was the saliva and sloppiness of it.

We dated on and off, but we broke up one year later.

'bye.

My second relationship's first kiss was pretty disappointing, too.

2nd boyfriend →

He fainted, and I felt bad. That was our basic relationship for 3 years.

We eventually went our separate ways.

Sorry...

After those 2 first kisses, I thought maybe love wasn't real. Maybe the fairy tales were wrong.

Maybe it's just something we believed in to make the world more interesting, like Santa Claus.

Maybe it's just nature's way to trick us into making babies.

oops!

SIGH.

Maybe I'll grow up to be an old maid with 21 cats.

Then I had breakfast in Hawaii with my mom and bro...

(25 yrs with new haircut)

When are you gonna get married?

Marriage?

I'd never thought about that before.

CHEW CHEW

Isn't marriage about society enforcing people into neat, domestic roles?

Remember dreaming about those first kisses when you were little?

Remember fantasizing about a loving, caring husband who'd treat you like a princess? And in return you'd treat him like your prince?

Remember?

Hey... that "prince" looks like my friend Kazu.

Why does he look like Kazu?!

And it looks like we have three kids. We look...

happy.

The time came to try my third "first kiss." The one that would test the vision of my future with Kazu!

SPRIT! SPRIT!

But first, a brief backstory:

Kazu and I were comic book colleagues, and we often chatted until morning.

TAP TAP

TAP TAP

And so, on a subway platform on our way from the airport, we silently shared our first kiss:

Our hearts fluttered,

and our spirits soared.

We were whole, at last.

It was a magical first kiss, just like the ones in my dreams.

The next day, we made plans to marry each other.

A year later, he officially proposed in Hawaii.

Two years later...

We had a real wedding.

And best of all—

to this day, each kiss feels just as wonderful as the first!

The end

Amy Kim Ganter is the creator of Tokyopop's two-part romantic comic *Sorcerers & Secretaries,* as well as a contributor to the Flight anthologies published by Vallard. On the side she runs her art site, www.felaxx.com. Amy lives in California with her husband, Kazu Kibuishi, who is also a graphic novelist.

Shannon and Dean Hale

Our First Kiss
(with each other)

Her Version

Dean and I had become friends when I was fifteen. Man, I dug that boy. He was so smart, so funny, so strong, and I was pretty sure I was the only one in the world who really got how amazing he was. But he, sadly, was also shockingly ignorant of my own stellar qualities and thought of me as no more than a friend for *far* too long. It's taken many years for him to live down this deplorable lack of insight, and I still need to remind him of it occasionally, just to keep him in line. You understand.

He graduated high school two years ahead of me and went to college out of state. And then followed the Untouchable Age. For the next six years, we were either living in separate states, countries, or dating someone else. All that time we remained good friends—letter writing, phoning (no e-mail yet—yes, I know, I'm ancient), and if you've ever had a best friend of the opposite sex, you'll understand my general anxiety. No, I don't love him anymore, I told myself again and again. He doesn't love me. I got over him years ago. We're just friends. No romance about it. Zip.

And then . . . I'm twenty-two. We both find ourselves living in Utah again. Both unattached. My heart yearned and mourned him so intensely in years past, I don't dare risk that pain again. And yet . . . and yet, could something happen? Could the Friends Barrier be broken and Romance triumph?

He's at my parents' house one night. We are sitting next to each other on the couch, watching *Star Wars* with my sister. We are sitting closer. And closer. The movie ends—much too soon.

"Uh, you guys want to watch *The Empire Strikes Back* now?" I ask, not wanting to give up this spot on the couch next to him.

"Yeah," he says. "Let's do."

We put in the next movie. And my sister (oblivious) stays. Curse her.

Near the end, she yawns, half asleep, and goes to bed. But we don't move. We're holding hands now. And my mind is still justifying, still thinking, It doesn't mean anything. His hands are just cold. We're just cuddling friends. That's all.

We watch the credits. The screen goes to static, and still neither of us moves or says a word. I snuggle in tighter, putting my head on his chest. I can feel his heart beating so hard, my head bounces.

Then he's kissing my head, my hair. Panic fills me like ice water, and I think, "What's happening? Have his feelings for me really changed, or is it just a spontaneous moment that he'll regret later? And if we admit we're not just friends anymore, will our romance be brief and destroy our friendship? Will one kiss ruin everything?"

Then the other side of my brain (which is, apparently, British) says, "Screw the insecurity. I have got to snog this bloke."

I turn my face up, and we kiss, on and off for about half an hour. Mmm, he's luscious.

Four years later, we marry.

Ever since, we've always told people our song is "The Imperial March." When I call Dean's cell from the home phone, that song is his ringtone. His coworkers think it's a funny way of referring to me as Darth Vader, but I know the (unlikely and actually quite romantic) truth. Oh yes, I know.

His Version

The girl with whom I shared my first Kiss* was a witch. Not the evil stab-you-in-the-back heartless

* There are kisses, and then there are Kisses. When someone says "Heidi Devlin of the Innsmouth Devlins was my first kiss," they're usually talking about their first Kiss. Capital K. Because your first kiss, little k, was probably your mother or, if I recall the event correctly, a greedy-lipped pediatric nurse.

harpy kind, but the mix-potions-to-bend-your-will kind.

You think I'm kidding, but let me outline my evidence.

I have no memory of what led up to my first Kiss. None. I don't remember how I got to her house, how I ended up sitting next to her on the couch, and why I thought staying there for six hours in the deep of night seemed like a good idea. I just don't remember. At all.

I remember the Kiss itself fine. Somehow we found ourselves watching the entire Star Wars trilogy. I don't think I started out sitting next to her, which, in retrospect, seems pretty rude, but there you go. The point is, by the time *The Empire Strikes Back* started, I was sitting next to her. And after two hours and four minutes of fruity-smelling hair, her soft breathing next to me, and the concentrated onslaught of compatible hormones, I was not only ready to kiss this girl, I was ready to *devour her*. (I didn't devour her, of course. It would have been messy and improper.) My heart was beating like I'd followed up an afternoon of wind sprints with twelve espressos. Her hair and skin smelled and felt angelic. At some point, our lips met and it was perhaps the most wonderful thing I'd ever experienced. And truly, I guess there wasn't just one kiss, but several. A polite frenzy. A mass migration of delicate wildebeest kisses. I remember them as one transcendent event, though. Each kiss working with the next to form a single thing. If there was such a thing as a bunny hive, I'd say that was what it was like. As there isn't, I'll spare myself the embarrassment.

I don't believe there was tongue, so don't ask.

But see, I don't remember anything after that. Before or after. How did I get home? When did I get home? No idea. And no, alcohol was not involved. At the time, I took great pride in my tee-totaling clarity of thought.

This girl and I, who weren't dating before, suddenly were. And seriously. It took me only a few weeks to be certain I wanted to marry her. And then I did marry her. Oh, it took four years for her serial hexing to actually take hold and get that proverbial knot tied, but I always knew it was inevitable.

And before you write me off as a simple forgetful paranoiac, explain this to me—she tells everyone that she loved me for years. Ever since high school. She says she loved me desperately and showed it in every way she could, but I was a clueless turd who wouldn't even give her a pity date. I remember none of this. I remember her from high school. I remember we were friends. I remember thinking she was cute. I even remember thinking I should ask her out. I have absolutely no recollection of spurning her. So here's the thing: either I have a fundamentally unbalanced mind and have remanufactured my own history in a completely random way, *or* she cast a spell on me.

Which do *you* think is more likely? Occam's razor, baby. Occam's razor.

Anyway, for all you witches out there, just be careful who you ensorcell. If you're undeniably beautiful, intelligent, and the best friend anyone could ever have (like my witch is), you might just end up married to a hopelessly devoted turd.

Shannon and Dean Hale married in 2000 and have remained best friends despite the kissing. Dean is Shannon's biggest fan and has been an essential in-home editor on Shannon's six books, including the Newbery Honor book and bestseller *Princess Academy* and the recently released *Book of a Thousand Days.* Together they coproduced two stunning children and cowrote two stunning graphic novels (the first, *Rapunzel's Revenge,* will be out this year). More at www.shannonhale.com.

Nikki Grimes

Breathless

Santiago held me

in the suave curve

of his bony brown arms,

showing off his fourteen-year-old

ways of the world

by moving toward my lips

in TV slo-mo.

I squeezed my eyes tight

and leaned forward,

feigning experience,

not knowing my pursed lips

gave me away.

His hot tongue startled me,

torching its way in where

it wasn't needed.

(Didn't I already have

a tongue of my own?)

All that weird rolling around

the dark cavern of my mouth,

an intimacy routinely reserved

for my toothbrush,

made me ready to gasp, or gag—

I couldn't tell which.

And right there and then,

smack in the middle of the kiss

I found myself wondering:

Is this what they mean by

taking your breath away?

Nikki Grimes is the recipient of the 2006 NCTE Award for Excellence in Poetry for Children. Her distinguished works include ALA Notable book *What Is Goodbye?* and the novels *Jazmin's Notebook, Dark Sons,* and *The Road to Paris* (Coretta Scott King Author Honor Books). Creator of the popular Meet Danitra Brown, Ms. Grimes lives in Corona, California.

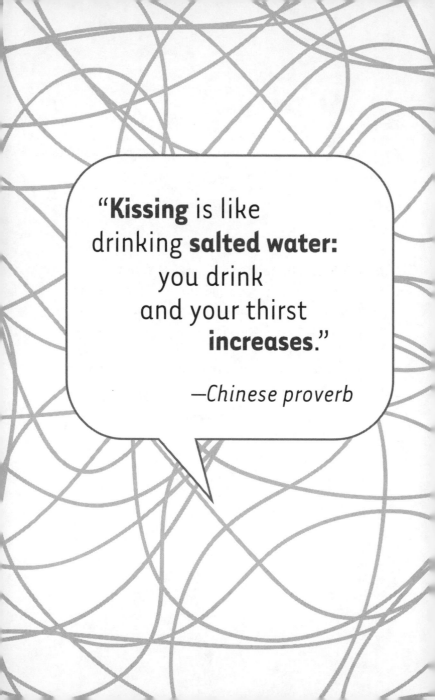

"**Kissing** is like drinking **salted water:** you drink and your thirst **increases**."

—Chinese proverb

Lisa
Papademetriou

You Can Take
the Girl Out
of Texas . . .

"Hey, Lisa," Jim said as he, Tami, and I paddled around the small lake at the edge of camp. We were in red kayaks, and Jim had one heel trailing in the water. "Hey Lisa," Jim repeated as he paddled a little closer. "Would you ever consider going with Payton?"

"Are you serious?" I asked, sweeping my paddle into the water at the side of my boat in order to turn around. I remember being amazed at how easy a kayak is to handle. I'd never been in one before, and the exotic word "kayak" had made me very nervous. A lot of things at this camp made me nervous. For one thing, it was in Vermont. I was born and raised in Texas, but this particular summer—the summer I was thirteen—my father was getting remarried to a woman from New York. For some reason, he thought it would be a good idea for me to go to this expensive camp full of kids from New York City and—yes, I'm totally serious—one Norwegian exchange student named Lars. This camp was so fancy that one of the campers was the child of a Beatle. Parents' Day was a parade of people I'd seen on TV.

Meanwhile, I was a kid from Houston who lived in a ranch house with my single mom. The New York girls had exotic names like "Noelle" and "Arielle" and beautiful, long curly hair. My hair, on the other hand, was short at the back but long enough in the front to occasionally get stuck in my braces. The other girls had wardrobes from Benetton and Esprit; I had clothes from Marshalls. The other girls had coordinating Laura Ashley blankets and sheets; I had an old green army blanket and a duffel bag with my dad's name written on it. Everyone else knew how to sneak candy bars and soda into the camp, while the healthy yogurt-covered raisins that my grandmother sent were confiscated by the counselors before they even hit my bunk. I could go on and on, but I think you get the picture.

Nobody was mean to me, but I was absolutely not the most desirable girl in camp. Which was why all of the other girls had boyfriends to kiss at night, while I had a pillow.

"Payton White?" I narrowed my eyes at Jim. "Why are you asking?"

Jim shrugged. "He likes you."

"He does?" I asked.

"He does?" Tami asked, angling herself closer to us.

"Sure." Jim placed his double-edged paddle across his lap and looked at me with disarming brown eyes. Jim had a rectangular head, like a shoe box, but his quick smile and honesty made his weird looks seem cute. He was a nice guy—

maybe even crushworthy—but that didn't matter now, because Payton White liked me.

"Ooh!" Tami looked at me with huge eyes.

"I think you and Payton would be a rockin' couple," Jim went on.

"You do? Why?" Payton wasn't exactly my ideal guy. No, my ideal guy was named Matt. He had blond hair and blue eyes and was going with Charlotte, one of the most beautiful girls in my cabin, if not the world.

Payton, on the other hand, was built solidly— like a well-packed snowman. He had creamy skin, pink cheeks, and green eyes. He sounds kind of dreamy when I describe him, but he'd definitely never entered my dreams before. "Why would we be rockin'?" I asked Jim.

"Well, because you're rockin'"—Jim thought it over—"and he's rockin'."

"Really?" I asked. This was because I thought that most people hated Payton. He was known for making loud belching noises, and had once managed to set the boys' cabin on fire. It was a small fire, but still. He did it by making a flamethrower out of his aerosol deodorant and a cigarette lighter.

I didn't know him well, but he didn't seem very rockin' to me. It struck me that perhaps I'd misjudged him. After all, Jim was someone I liked. And he thought that I was rockin'. If I was rockin' and Payton was rockin'—well, that must mean we had *something* in common.

Naturally, though, no decision could be made without discussing the situation with my best girlfriends.

"Go for it," said my best friend, Elyssa, when I got back to the cabin. "Why not? Payton's a nice guy."

"I thought you said he was a horrible jerk," I told her.

"I didn't mean it," she insisted.

"He can be annoying," Gia said honestly. "But he can be funny, too."

"He's funny," Elyssa said. "You're funny. Why not?"

I knew what she was thinking—it wasn't like I

had a lot of options. Elyssa was going with a tall, slim artist type named Sam, and Gia was dating Lars, who we all referred to as the Swedish Pancake, even though he was from Norway. Come to think of it, Payton had given him that nickname. I had serious doubts that my version of funny and his would mesh, but Elyssa had a point—I didn't have a lot of options.

And so I told Jim to tell Payton yes. Yes, I would sit with him at the next campfire. I would meet him beforehand. He should bring the blanket.

We were both shy when we met at the edge of the campfire. But Payton smelled extra nice, I noticed, and his hair was brushed. I wondered if he was wearing his flamethrowing deodorant.

We sat through the campfire songs, both muttering along with the words, too self-conscious to really sing along. Then it was over, and we were left alone at the center of confusion as campers milled around, forming small clumps to trek back to the cabins. Payton gathered up the blanket, and we started our walk toward The Woods.

The Woods was a small knot of trees near the boys' cabin. It was where all the kids who were going together Made Out. As we walked toward the woods, my stomach felt queasy with fear. What was he going to expect? What if I was a lousy kisser? Was he going to tell everyone in the cabin that I had chapped lips? What if he tried to feel my boobs? There have been only a few times in my life when I have felt as unprepared as I did at that moment.

He came to a stop in the shadow of a pine. Flashlights danced like fireflies as campers streamed past thirty feet away from us, beyond the trees. I heard a laugh to my right and realized that Gia and the Swedish Pancake were nearby.

This is really happening, I thought. *I'm going to kiss Payton White!* I didn't particularly care about the kiss, but I wanted—for once—to have the same thing that all of the other girls in my cabin had. I wanted to be able to use the words "my boyfriend," and gossip about my own life, for a change. Maybe I couldn't have a Laura Ashley comforter, but I could have this.

I felt a hand at my waist, then smelled warm, minty breath, and in a moment his lips were on mine. They were soft. Then something squishy and slug-like pressed past my lips. A tongue—I was French kissing! Whoa.

I barely had time to absorb this before Payton pulled away. "Good night," he said.

"Good night," I said.

He disappeared into the darkness of the trees, and at the next moment, I heard a voice by my ear. "Did you kiss him?" It was Gia.

"Yeah," I said.

"How was it?" she asked.

Squishy, I thought. *Weird.* But what I said was "Good. I guess."

She giggled, and slung a casual arm around my shoulders as we walked back to our cabin. "Elyssa's going to want to hear all about it," Gia said as our footsteps fell into an easy rhythm.

In the distance, I saw our cabin. Light spilled from the windows, and I could just make out the other girls moving around inside. Laughter floated out the front door, like a spark from a fire, fading into the cool night air. I imagined Elyssa inside, waiting to hear about my evening at the campfire with Payton. All of the girls would want to hear about it. Good or gross, magical or slimy—it didn't matter.

Finally, I had a story to share.

Lisa Papademetriou is the author of many novels, including *Sixth-Grade Glommers, Norks, and Me*; *The Wizard, the Witch, and Two Girls from Jersey*; *How to Be a Girly Girl in Just Ten Days*; and the forthcoming *Chasing Normal*. She lives in Northampton, Massachusetts, with her husband and adorable dog. For more about Lisa, check out her Web site: www.lisapapa.com.

Paul Ruditis

Improvisation

A Dramatic Reenactment . . .
with a little poetic license

The time is 1989. The setting is a rec room in a middle-class home in a middle-class neighborhood in middle-class America. An old couch sits against the wood-paneled wall where a poster of the movie Heathers *hangs at an angle. Paula Abdul's "Straight Up" plays softly as the light rises. Two boys costumed in street clothes—jeans, a Depeche Mode T-shirt or a polo, Chucks—stand a few feet apart, each holding a paperback book with the cover bent back. They are rehearsing a scene from* Romeo and Juliet.

ROMEO: *(Reading)* Give me a torch. I am not for

this ambling. Being but heavy, I will bear the light.

MERCUTIO: But soft! What light through yonder window breaks?

ROMEO: That's the wrong part of the play.

MERCUTIO: I'm improvising.

ROMEO: Well, knock it off. Ms. Greenberg isn't grading on improvisation. She's grading on memorization. You want to improvise, join the drama club. We've got to get this scene down. *(Reading)* . . . Being but heavy. I will bear the light.

MERCUTIO: *(Laughs)*

ROMEO: What?

MERCUTIO: You said you're "butt heavy."

ROMEO: Come on!

MERCUTIO: I'm sorry. I'm sorry. *(Reading)* Nay, gentle Romeo, we must have you dance. *(He sways to the music, moving closer to Romeo)*

ROMEO: *(Reading)* Not I, believe me. You have dancing shoes with nimble soles. I have . . .

What are you doing? Get off me! *(He pushes Mercutio away)*

MERCUTIO: I was dancing. Like the script says.

ROMEO: The script does not say Mercutio dances with Romeo.

MERCUTIO: It's implied.

ROMEO: No. No, it's not implied. It's stupid. Romeo and Mercutio do not suddenly start dancing together. Will you stop messing around!

MERCUTIO: Sorry. *(Reading)* You are a lover. Borrow cupid's wings and soar with them above a common ground.

Romeo says nothing. He stares at Mercutio.

MERCUTIO: What?

ROMEO: *(Shakes it off)* Nothing. That was . . . very Harrison Ford.

MERCUTIO: Really? Han Solo or Indiana Jones?

ROMEO: Han Solo all the way . . . you know, if he spoke Shakespeare.

MERCUTIO: Cool. We totally have to see *Last Crusade.*

ROMEO: Definitely. *(Reading)* Not I, believe me. You—

MERCUTIO: We did that part.

ROMEO: Oh? Oh, yeah. Um . . .

MERCUTIO: You are too sore . . .

ROMEO: I am?

MERCUTIO: That's the line.

ROMEO: *(Reading)* I am too sore enpierced with . . . Okay, I don't have a clue what's going on in this scene.

MERCUTIO: *(Laughs)* Dude, it's not that hard. Mercutio is trying to get his best friend to live a little. Romeo has all these grand ideas about romantic love, but Mercutio just wants him to have some fun. Stop being so dramatic. Let his guard down and see what happens.

ROMEO: Someone's done their research.

MERCUTIO: *(Pause)* You know . . . Shakespeare scholars have suggested that Mercutio had a thing for his best friend. That they were maybe more than friends.

ROMEO: Been reading many Shakespeare scholars?

MERCUTIO: I looked some stuff up when I picked the scene.

ROMEO: I think you're reading too much into this play.

MERCUTIO: Not me. The Shakespeare scholars.

ROMEO: *(Nodding)* Right. Shakespeare scholars.

MERCUTIO: I mean, he effectively dies for his best friend. I'd do that.

ROMEO: You'd die for me?

MERCUTIO: *(Playfully)* Wouldn't you die for me?

ROMEO: *(Playing along)* I might kill you. Especially if we blow this scene tomorrow.

MERCUTIO: *(Laughs)* Nice. I tell you I'd die for you and your response is to threaten my life. That's some thanks!

ROMEO: Okay. Fine. I'd die for you.

MERCUTIO: Really?

ROMEO: Well, I wouldn't take a sword to the

gut, but maybe I'd donate a kidney. I'd undergo invasive surgery for you.

MERCUTIO: Doesn't sound quite as romantic.

ROMEO: If you wanted a love scene you should have picked a girl for your partner.

MERCUTIO: I didn't want to do a scene with a girl. I wanted to do a scene with you.

ROMEO: Oh.

There is an awkward pause.

MERCUTIO: *(Reading slowly. With uncertainty.)* And to sink in it, should you burthen love. Too great oppression for a tender thi—

Romeo suddenly kisses Mercutio.

Mercutio's eyes go wide in surprise, but he doesn't pull away. He kisses back. It is awkward and rushed and comfortable and perfect.

They finally break.

MERCUTIO: That was definitely not in the script.

ROMEO: I was improvising.

Paul Ruditis is the author of the teen series Drama!, which includes the books *The Four Dorothys* and *Everyone's a Critic*. He has also written and contributed to numerous books based on popular TV shows like *Buffy the Vampire Slayer, Charmed, Prison Break,* and *Bones*.

Kisses
on the Silver Screen

First ever on-screen kiss: In a movie suitably called *The Kiss* (1896). People were offended and called for the film to be censored.

Largest number of kisses in a film: 191, in *Don Juan* (1926). The film's star, John Barrymore, performed every one of those lip-exhausting smooches.

First male-male kiss on the lips: *Wings* (1927). It was between friends — as one of them was dying.

First female-female kiss on the lips: *Morocco* (1930). It was quite scandalous at the time.

First kiss in a full-length animated film: *Snow White and the Seven Dwarfs* (1937). Not only did Snow White receive a kiss from her Prince Charming, but she also planted pecks on all seven of the dwarfs. Of course, arguably the most famous animated movie kiss is from another Disney film, *Lady and the Tramp* (1955) in which a strand of spaghetti leads to an accidental meeting of the lips between two star-crossed pooches.

Longest kiss: Regis Toomey and Jane Wyman's kiss in *You're in the Army Now* (1941). It clocked in at just over three minutes!

Most iconic kiss: Burt Lancaster and Deborah Kerr's kiss in the film, *From Here to Eternity* (1953). While the two embraced on a sandy beach, the ocean waves came crashing over them. Even people who have never seen the movie can picture the scene.

"Best ever" kiss: Wesley and Buttercup in *The Princess Bride* (1987). As the narrator says, it's the most passionate kiss of all time.

Sweetest first kiss: Macaulay Culkin and Anna Chlumsky in *My Girl* (1991). This kiss between childhood friends was the first to win an MTV Movie Award for Best Kiss.

"Worst ever" kiss: *Casino* (1995). This kiss between Sharon Stone and Joe Pesci earned that dubious title in a vote by the readers of *Film* magazine.

And finally, the first kiss upside-down, in the rain, between a woman and a superhero suspended on a spiderweb: *Spider-Man* (2002), with Tobey Maguire and Kirsten Dunst.

"**Kissing**—
and I mean like,
yummy, smacking kissing—
is the most **delicious,**
most **beautiful** and
passionate thing that
two people can do,
bar none."

—*Drew Barrymore*

Sarah Mlynowski and Leslie Margolis

Read Our Lips

Kissing Advice from Sarah and Leslie

Sarah Mlynowski and Leslie Margolis have kissed a boy or two over the years. (But as far as they know, never the same one.) Now they're sharing their wisdom with you.

DEAR SARAH & LESLIE: Help! My boyfriend and I tried to kiss and now our braces are locked together. What do I do?

—BRACE FACED IN BRIDGEPORT

DEAR BRACE FACED: Before you call the orthodontist or pull out the blowtorch, think about this: if this guy is your boyfriend, you must adore him. And now you're stuck together? Be honest. Is it really all that terrible? Think about the quality time you two will now have. And what about the fact that you'll never have to deal with another teary-eyed goodbye? Have you ever had to choose between your friends and your boyfriend? Well, those days are over. Now you won't need to decide between your guy and anything, because he'll always be there, right by your side. Er, right in front of your face.

Anyway, wouldn't you rather have your *boyfriend* stuck in your teeth than, say, a piece of spinach? So rather than see yourself as a victim of some major metallic mistake, consider yourself lip-locked and lucky.

♥   ♥   ♥

DEAR SARAH & LESLIE: I'm having my

first ever grown-up, boy/girl party in a couple of weeks and I want to play Spin the Bottle. Do you have any advice?

—PARTY GIRL IN PORTLAND

DEAR PARTY GIRL: Absolutely. First off, as you must know, there is a raging debate over whether a Coke bottle or a Pepsi bottle works best. Some people swear by Sprite, but our top choice is generic seltzer. Just make sure the empty bottle didn't contain tangerine-flavored seltzer, or all types of chaos will ensue. Second, dim the lights. That way, if you have to kiss someone who isn't cute, you won't notice as much. Third, tie a strand of dental floss around the nape of bottle and keep the end hidden in the palm of your hand. If your spin lands on someone you're just not that into, simply give the floss a tug until the bottle points to the boy of your dreams. If anyone accuses you of cheating, remind them that it's your party and you make the rules. Friends love it when you play that card.

❤   ❤   ❤

DEAR SARAH & LESLIE: How do I get my crush to kiss me? Do you know any kissing potions?
—READY TO SMOOCH IN RAPID CITY

DEAR READY: Of course we do! First, go collect these ingredients:

1 cup coffee
1 teaspoon garlic powder
¼ cup chopped onion

DIRECTIONS
1. The day before you want the kiss to take place, pour some of your mom's coffee into a tall glass.

2. Drop in garlic powder.

3. Add onion.

4. Stir.

5. Let sit all day.

6. Before bed, sip concoction. Gargle. Swallow. Chew on remaining chunks. Swallow.

7. Go straight to sleep. Do not brush teeth.

8. Upon waking, still do not brush teeth.

9. Locate your crush. Ignore all gagging facial expressions. The potion is working! He'll be moving in for the kiss any moment. All you have to do is wait . . . and wait . . . and wait . . .

Wait a sec. Something looks off about the recipe. We may have made a teeny-tiny mistake in there. Maybe you're supposed to shake instead of stir? Um . . . we'll get back to you on that one, 'kay?

♥ ♥ ♥

DEAR SARAH & LESLIE: Yikes! My boyfriend kissed me, and my gum kind of fell into his mouth. What do I do?

—**CHEWED UP AND SPIT OUT IN CHATTANOOGA**

DEAR CHEWED UP: What do you do? Thank your boyfriend for doing you a huge favor. You know how gum tastes good only for an hour or so before it loses its flavor? Well, your boyfriend displayed thoughtfulness and generosity by taking that gum off your hands. This guy is a definite keeper.

Unless you'd just popped that piece of gum into your mouth. In that case, he obviously kissed you so he could steal it, and you must break up with him immediately. That gum was yours and you cannot let boys steal from you.

♥ ♥ ♥

DEAR SARAH & LESLIE: I think my boyfriend is finally going to kiss me! Yay! What can I do to make sure I'm ready?   **—WAITING IN WORCESTER**

DEAR WAITING: What's your most important kissing muscle? No, not your heart—your lips! (Fine, we're not entirely sure lips have muscles, but give us a break, we're not doctors.) Anyway, what do you do with muscles? You exercise them! There is only one lip exercise guaranteed to work. Here is the beginner's and advanced version: (*Important*—do not try the advanced unless you have mastered the beginner's. Trust us. Unless you're going for the Donald Duck look.)

> **Beginner:** *The Pucker.* Go to a mirror. Pucker up. Release. Pucker up again. Release. Repeat twenty times.

> **Advanced:** *Speed Puckering.* Time

yourself. Aim for one hundred per minute. Stop when you can no longer feel your lips.

Once you get the hang of these exercises, you can do them anywhere! You don't even need the mirror. What a great way to use your wasted time. Bored on the bus? Drifting off in Bio? Pucker away. If people stare or laugh at you, just ignore them. Sure, you may look silly, but what is more important? Your social status or your first kiss?

Exactly.

What? Your boyfriend is in Bio with you? And now he's afraid of you? Oh.

Better luck next time!

❤ ❤ ❤

DEAR SARAH & LESLIE: Okay, this is bad. The guy I have a major crush on tried to kiss me last night. Tried is the key word here, because as soon as he leaned in, I felt a weird tickle inside my nose, and before I knew it, I sneezed in his face. Not to be gross or anything, but it was a wet sneeze. I've been avoiding him ever since, but I can't keep it up forever. What do I do?

   —BOO-HOO ACHOO IN HONOLULU

DEAR BOO-HOO: There's a simple solution. Tell your parents you must move to another country, immediately. Make sure this country is far from home, and that no one there speaks your native language. That way, your story will never get out.

(A note from the editor: on the other hand, you're probably better off NOT *following any of Sarah and Leslie's advice.)*

Sarah Mlynowski has written three novels for teens (*Bras & Broomsticks*, *Frogs & French Kisses*, and *Spells & Sleeping Bags*), and six books for adults. She is currently working on a new novel called *How to Be Bad* with YA writers Lauren Myracle and E. Lockhart. Originally from Montreal, Sarah now lives in New York City. She'd love to hear from you—say hello at www.sarahm.com.

Leslie Margolis is the author of *Fix*, *Price of Admission*, and the forthcoming *Boys Are Dogs*. She lives, writes, and occasionally teaches in Brooklyn, New York. To find out more about Leslie and her books, please visit www.lesliemargolis.com.

Robin Wasserman

Public Service Announcement

You didn't notice him, not at first. Not until you noticed him noticing you.

Your best friend went out with his best friend, which left him stuck with you by default. He didn't seem to mind. He smiled and teased and tossed you nicknames and, one winter day, threw you into the snow, which is when you decided that, against all reason, he must be flirting—and although you weren't sure how to flirt back, you did what you could. Mostly, you blushed.

You weren't his type.

You knew this because he spent most of your time together talking about other girls, the ones who *were* his type—pretty and polished and perfectly feminine, with shimmery eye shadow and manicured toenails. Tan, leggy girls with skirts that offered a hint of thigh, girls who giggled girlishly, pouting glossy lips when denied what they wanted, which was rarely, if ever. He preferred blondes to brunettes and brunettes to redheads, though you had no idea how he felt about your own hair, a dirty mix of all three, like the muddy gunk left on a paintbrush at the end of art class. You knew exactly who he wanted and how much and why, because he had composed a list, ranking all the possibilities, shuffling girls' names around from day to day like the ever-changing brackets in his NCAA betting tree, slowly but surely narrowing in on a final four.

You weren't on it.

But that didn't matter, not when you were the one he called in the middle of the night when he couldn't fall asleep. His giggly blondes didn't know how to listen, and they couldn't make him laugh, while you always could, even when—especially when—he was laughing at you and the way your cheeks reddened under his stare. His kind of girl counted calories; you chewed on a shared slice of pizza—pretending to like pepperoni because *he* liked pepperoni—while he debated who he should ask out, and how. Beneath the table, you drove the jagged edge of your house key into the palm of your hand so you wouldn't have to think about what he was saying and, as he listed one name after another, weighing pros and cons and measurements, you focused on the pain, and nodded and smiled as if you didn't care.

You were willing to be patient. And more than willing to change. You learned to wear contact lenses; you painted your toenails pink. Your friends didn't get it, because they didn't get *him*, but you did, and that made everything worth it—everything you did, everything you became. Even if it meant no more gnawed cuticles and no more frizzy hair. Or wearing tank tops with accessories to match, laughing at his bad jokes, watching Harrison Ford movies and agreeing with him that yes, he was just as bold as Indiana, just as brave as Han Solo, buffer and brainier than Jack Ryan and Richard Kimble combined. You pretended to care whether the Packers beat the Patriots or the Cowboys beat the Dolphins; you pretended not to care that his e-mails were incoherent, because the important thing was that he keep sending them.

You pretended. Every day you pretended, terrified of what would happen if anyone found out, if anyone suspected that you imagined a possibility, a remote, unlikely, infinitely small but still technically possible possibility. Because you knew what would happen next: they would laugh. And then, worse, they would tell him.

And you would die.

You warned yourself not to expect anything to happen, since you were the kind of person that only nothing ever happened to. But if you couldn't expect, you could still hope.

There was the night he called just to say hello, and it seemed like he had something he wanted say—something he wanted to *ask*—and a dance was coming up, and even though you knew better you couldn't help wondering . . . but then he said good night and hung up, and the next day he asked someone else. There was the day his shoulders were sore, and your best friend, who never guessed how hard you were pretending—even she couldn't be allowed to know—gave him a massage, like it was nothing. Because for her it *was* nothing, and for him it was nothing, and you sat there hating yourself for being afraid to touch and for being jealous and for staying and watching when all you wanted to do was leave.

You always stayed. Just in case something happened.

Nothing happened.

Nothing ever happened.

And then—

It was late, so late it was almost early. The party died and everyone left, but you stayed—you stayed because he asked you to, and because when he asked, you were lying on the couch with your head nestled into the hollow of his neck and his fingers woven through your hair, straying toward your face, toward your skin, and his other hand was flat against your stomach, where you could feel his warmth even through the thin fabric of your shirt. They left you there alone with him in the dark, and he traced his fingers from your forehead to your chin, and you shivered and waited for something to interrupt, for this something to turn back into nothing.

You almost ran away.

You couldn't catch your breath. You couldn't make your arms stop shaking. He smirked, and asked why your heart was beating so fast, and brushed his fingers across the back of your neck, which made you jump away, but he caught you, and when he asked if you wanted to leave, you just shook your head, because you couldn't get out the word.

You didn't see his face move toward you in the

dark. You felt his lips. You tasted his tongue. You tensed as his palm crept up your lower back, and he jerked it away, and you were sorry, but you still couldn't speak, so you couldn't tell him what you wanted, and he guessed wrong. He stopped. But then lips met again. Fingers twined, skin touched skin. He held you, and you breathed together, and then, too soon, he let go.

And it was over.

And you left.

Now you worry that you made a mistake. Many mistakes: letting him stop. Letting him think you wanted him to stop. Or maybe not stopping sooner. Maybe kissing him at all. Because now he knows how much you *don't* know. He knows how much you've been pretending, and he'll never want to kiss you again.

Or else he will.

And then what?

You tell yourself not to panic. This is what you wanted. You wanted *him*. You wanted the night, and his lips, and whatever comes next, and surely something will, because that is how it works for other people, and you want to believe you are now officially one of the other people, the ones who get what they want, the ones who live in your TV and beam at you from magazine spreads and brush past you in the halls holding hands, the ones who have forgotten that it was ever any other way, although you have promised yourself you will never forget, no matter how much you might want to. You tell yourself you are just like them, even though they never look scared. Even though you are terrified.

You curl up on your couch and stare out the window, which just happens to be next to the phone, only a coincidence because you are *not* looking at the phone, *not* waiting for it to ring. Thinking about the phone—thinking about him—is off-limits, because that can only lead to thinking about what happened, which makes it hard to breathe. But it's impossible *not* to think about what it will be like when you see him next, if things will be different, and if they are not different, if everything is the same, what it will mean, if it will mean anything. If anything meant anything.

It did, you tell yourself.

It had to.

This is not like the other times, with the other girls. *You* are not other girls. And the kiss would never have happened—he would never have let it happen—if it hadn't meant something. Because he knows it would mean something to you.

And you know he would never be that cruel.

You stare at the phone and worry that he will call, and what it will mean, and when he does call—*if* he does call—what you will have to do next.

You worry that he won't.

He won't.

Robin Wasserman is the author of *Hacking Harvard*, the Seven Deadly Sins series, and the Chasing Yesterday trilogy. She grew up in Philadelphia and now lives in New York. Her second kiss went better than the first.

Roz Chast

My First Kiss(es)

My First Kiss(es)

My first kiss took place when I was about twelve.

NO. DOESN'T COUNT. YES!

I was sitting on the hood of a parked car with one of the boys. It felt a little dangerous, like we were juvenile delinquents.

The most exciting part was thinking to myself, as I went back up to my apartment, "A boy kissed me."

!!! ???

The world actually spun. I thought I might FAINT!

I was hanging out with my friend Gail who lived in my building.
ME
GAIL

A few kids we didn't know came over. They seemed o.k., so we all hung out together.

We were talking about this 'n' that. Suddenly the boy I was sitting with asked, "Do you wanna kiss?" I said:
O.K.

We pressed our lips together for about two seconds. That was it.
PRESS...

My first REAL kiss happened when I was thirteen. I was walking home from school with my best friend and a boy I had a huge crush on.

I don't remember what led up to it, but he took me in his arms, leaned me back slightly, and KISSED ME.

Maybe it was because I was leaning back, or because I had my eyes closed...
A.
B.

...but I doubt it.
I LOVE HENRY B!!!
ACTUAL X-RAY OF HEART

Roz Chast was born in Brooklyn, New York. She began contributing cartoons to the *New Yorker* in 1978. Since then nearly one thousand of her cartoons have appeared in the magazine. Her latest books include a collection, *Theories of Everything: Selected, Collected, and Health-Inspected Cartoons 1978–2006,* and a children's book entitled *The Alphabet From A to Y with Bonus Letter Z!,* written by Steve Martin and illustrated by Roz Chast.

Naomi Shihab
Nye

Independence,
Missouri

My first kiss

was a miss.

Consider a bee

imagining a tasty blossom—

dipping down to

the bright yellow cap

of a detergent bottle

in a recycling tub—

seated between Ken and Randy

at a dumb movie in Independence, Missouri

I dreamed thin freckled Randy would swerve

slightly west and find my face.

But it was Ken, toward movie's end,

disoriented and clunky in the dark,

who grabbed me from the east

and planted a big one

on my exclamation.

Had he forgotten which side

the girl who really liked him

was on? I think she gave up

on him that night.

And I, shaken and disheveled,

had trouble facing either

of them, bozo Ken or gentle Randy,

my daily pals, after that.

First kiss? Chalk up one.

Not fun.

Naomi Shihab Nye's most recent books are *I'll Ask You Three Times, Are You OK?: Tales of Driving & Being Driven* and *Honeybee*, both from Greenwillow.

Readers' Poll
First Kisses

There is no normal or abnormal, correct or incorrect, right or wrong when it comes to your first kiss. You can spend hours planning out exactly how you want it to happen—at what time or place, at what stage in your life, or with whom. But the beauty of a kiss is that it's often unexpected—the perfect kiss just can't be planned. And people are different, too. We polled people to find out what their kissing experiences were like—and the answers just might surprise you!

How old were you when you received your first kiss?

6%	8 or younger
23%	9–12 years old
52%	13–15 years old
19%	16 or older

How many people have you kissed in your life?

33%	1-5 people
17%	6-10 people
23%	11-15 people
27%	Too many to count!

Justine Larbalestier

Pashin'

or

The Worst Kiss Ever*

Pash is short for *passion*. In Australia it means kissing someone with tongues and everything. It's both a verb: "Wanna pash?" and a noun: "That was the best pash ever."

This is a gross first kiss story. If your stomach is weak, I strongly advise you to skip it. Move on to the next story. I'm sure it's much more sweet and wholesome. You do not want to go where I am about to take you.

This isn't my first kiss story (to be honest I can't remember my first kiss). It belongs to a friend. Ordinarily I'd be suspicious of this story, but unlike me, this friend does not lie. She is a truth teller and first told me this story not long after it happened. I have never forgotten. Well, okay, I've never forgotten the *main* bit. I've completely forgotten all the bibs and bobs. The core of what follows is true; the rest I made up.

It happened at a party in Sydney, Australia. The first party my friend had been to (that didn't involve pesky parents). She—let's call her Gemma—was fifteen and had never been kissed. She had big hopes of achieving kissage that night because the boy she had an enormous crush on—we'll call him Tom—was going to be there and he had actually spoken to her at school the day before even though he was a year ahead of her. Admittedly, he had only asked if she knew where Ms. Leatherbarrow, one of the PE teachers, was, but he could have asked anyone and he chose her. Gemma was sure it was a sign.

She and her best friend—picking another random-yet-popular-in-Australia name—Kylie got together hours and hours before the party. They did each other's makeup. Then wiped off the clown faces and started over. ("I can't believe you drew a mustache on me!" "Why did you make my mouth look ginormous?") They swapped clothes and lippy and plans and ate violet crumbles and pizza.

They wound up wearing jeans and a nice top (Gemma in one of Kylie's and Kylie in one of Gemma's). That way they were dressed up, but not *too* dressed up. Naturally, when they got to the party, none of the boys were wearing anything that could be described as *too* dressed up or even *dressed up*. Not even *nice*. Most of them were in torn jeans and torn T-shirts. The boys'd skipped the dressed-up option altogether.

The house the party was in hadn't though. Despite there being girls and boys hanging off the furniture, the staircases, and the balconies, and dropping ash and spilling beer and pizza. Gemma had never seen such a dressed-up house. She wondered who lived there. They had to be really rich.

It was the biggest house she'd ever been in. The ceiling was so high you'd need a crane to change the lightbulbs. The back verandah had a view of the Harbour Bridge and Luna Park. There was a grand piano! Gemma had never seen a piano that big. Not up close. Two girls were playing "Chopsticks" and laughing. The piano made even "Chopsticks" sound kind of okay.

But Gemma couldn't find Tom anywhere. And then Kylie started talking with this other guy and Gemma was on her own and realized that the only people she knew there had either hooked up or were too mean to talk to her.

Music blasted on out of nowhere. Gemma couldn't see any speakers. She put her hands over her ears and slipped out onto the back verandah where it wasn't as ear breaking. "Chopsticks" was wiped out completely.

Someone handed her a beer from the cooler in the corner. The last time she'd tried it, she hadn't liked it. She popped off the top and had a sip. Still pretty foul with a nasty bitter aftertaste. But at least it gave her something to do. She watched the lights flashing at Luna Park. Her beer was already empty. She fished an alcoholic lemonade out of the cooler. It tasted heaps better than the beer.

"Did you see they've got a yacht?"

Gemma turned, but the tall boy was talking to Jessica Sutton-Brown, not to her. Jessica never spoke to Gemma at school even though they had pretty much all the same classes. She didn't think Gemma was cool enough. Or something. That was fine. Gemma didn't think Jessica was interesting enough.

"See that white thing down behind those trees?" he said, pointing. Gemma looked and saw glimpses of something big and white. She tried to imagine having a yacht moored off your backyard. Her backyard had a clothesline and her mum's herb garden.

Fireworks went off and the verandah got more crowded. Gemma liked fireworks. She sipped her drink and *ooh*ed and *aah*ed along with everyone else.

"You finished with that?" someone yelled in her ear.

She turned to see a pimply boy slightly taller than her. He took the now-empty lemonade from her, dropped it in a huge garbage bag, handed her an empty plastic cup from a big stack of them, and then poured a reddish brown drink into it.

"Thanks."

Things were floating in the liquid. Gemma hoped they were fruit. She took a very tentative sip. It was sweet and spicy and alcohol-y and very yummy. The lumps were fruit. "Mmmm," she said. "This is brilliant." But the boy was already pouring for someone else.

At the end of her third cup of yummy brown drink with floating fruit bits, Gemma decided it was time to search for Tom again. There were heaps more people than before. She had to hold her cup high and weave between them. The music didn't seem so loud anymore because the sound of everyone talking and yelling and dancing came close to drowning it out.

She passed Kylie under the stairs wedged so close to her boy that you could hardly tell who was who. It looked like they were trying to gobble up each other's faces. Gemma shuddered. It did not look like fun. Kylie's makeup was smeared. And the boy's T-shirt was practically torn off. Though, to be fair, it had been pretty torn to start with.

She did not find Tom. But someone found her. "I'm Davo," he said. "Wanna pash?" He was staring at her mouth.

Davo was much taller than Gemma. He had no pimples and was blond and tan. He looked like he knew how to surf.

Gemma said, "Sure."

Davo led her down the steps from the kitchen into the garden. There was a rock garden and lots of ferns and flowers everywhere. The house was so bright that Gemma could see pretty well. Everything was a bit wavery though. She wondered how long it took to make a garden like that. Must be really hard. Specially as it was so slopey.

"Nice garden."

"Yeah. My dad's really into it."

"Is this your house?"

"Yeah."

"It's a big house. Is that really a yacht through there?" At the bottom of the garden something large and white bobbed in the harbor. "Are your parents posh?"

"Yeah."

"Which?"

"It's a yacht and they're posh."

"Crap!" Gemma slipped and the slopiness made righting herself tricky. Davo grabbed her arm.

"You okay?"

"Yeah," Gemma said since it was her turn to say it.

"Stand here." Davo still had her arm. He pulled her down to the bottom of the garden, past the trees, and onto the jetty. Gemma had never been to a house that had a jetty at the end of the garden and a great big yacht moored to that jetty.

"That's a big yacht," she said. The jetty wasn't slopey like the garden, but it made up for it by swaying. Although she couldn't see the people on the balcony she could hear them talking, yelling, and the thump of the bass. She tried to follow some of what was being said, but the words were fuzzy. Or maybe she was.

"Less of a slope here," Davo said.

"Yup. It's a bit wobbly, but."

"Well, it is a jetty, isn't it?"

"Right," Gemma said, feeling stupid. That's what a jetty does—it floats.

"Let's pash then," Davo said, putting his arm around her waist.

"Righ—" Gemma started to say, but his tongue was already in her mouth. She wasn't quite sure what to do, so she put her tongue next to his. Then they did a kind of tongue fight—sort of like a thumb fight only in your mouth. It was a bit too swirly. Davo pushed his mouth hard into hers. Gemma wondered if she'd get bruised. She also wondered if this was what was meant by lip-locked. It wasn't as romantic as she had imagined.

They kept tongue fighting, and pressing their mouths together. Gemma started to feel dizzy what with having to breathe out of her nose, and the swaying of the jetty; then she had another feeling—a not good feeling. A swirling in parts of her that weren't her tongue.

She tried to pull away, but Davo just held her tighter, and got more frenetic with his tongue dueling. Gemma wondered how you decided who won a tongue war.

Then the not-good feeling pushed into feeling bad. Very bad.

Oh no, she thought, pulling away from Davo harder.

He wouldn't let her go.

Gemma chucked. She chundered. She let loose the brown fruit drink and the beer and lemonade and pizza and violet crumble and everything else that had been happily hanging out in her belly.

The vomit shot up into her throat and her mouth and because it had nowhere else to go it shot straight into Davo.

Now he let go of Gemma.

She staggered back, gasping and wiping her mouth, just in time for Davo to let loose all over the jetty and her shoes and the bottom of her nice jeans.

Davo chucked and chucked and then chucked

some more. The sight of it set Gemma off again.

When they were finished, Davo grabbed a hose and washed everything away into the harbor. He handed it to Gemma, who aimed it at her shoes and jeans. And then rinsed her mouth.

Without saying a word they walked back into the house.

Gemma found Kylie and said she was leaving. Kylie went home with her, asking a million times if she was okay. Gemma said she was. She did not tell anyone of the horror of her first kiss for several days.

She never saw Davo again.

Gemma didn't kiss anyone else for more than a year. Her second kiss was not with Tom, but it went a lot better than the first.

Justine Larbalestier is the author of the award-winning Magic or Madness trilogy. She is currently at work on a new novel about fairies. Justine was born and raised in Sydney, Australia, and divides her time between Sydney and New York City (with sojourns in Mexico, New Zealand, Thailand, and anywhere else that strikes her fancy). She is married to author Scott Westerfeld. www.justinelarbalestier.com

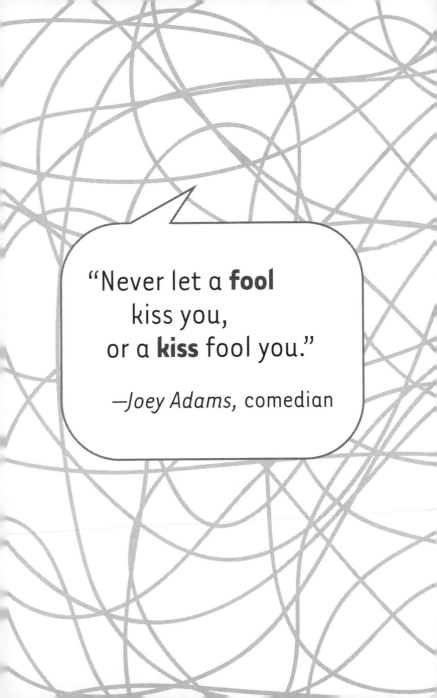

"Never let a **fool** kiss you, or a **kiss** fool you."

—*Joey Adams,* comedian

A Kiss Is Just
a Kiss

In **French,** a kiss is called *embrasser avec la langue,* literally "to kiss with tongue," although slang terms include *rouler une pelle* ("to roll a shovel") and *emballer* ("to pack").

In **Britain,** kissing is also called *snogging, pulling,* or *hooking up.*

In **Ireland,** it is most commonly called *meeting,* or also *shifting.*

In **India,** a kiss is referred to as an *English kiss.* This is because old Indian movies never showed passionate kissing, so it was only through British movies that Indians were exposed to such a practice.

In **Italy,** a kiss is referred to as *limonare,* or "to lemon."

In **Spanish,** it is called *morrear*—"to muzzle"— or *rumbear*—"to party."

In **Bosnia,** teens refer to French kissing as *Ïvaka,* which literally translates as "to bubble gum."

In **Australia** and **New Zealand,** it is referred to as *pashing,* probably originating from the idea of passion and passionate kissing.

In **Newfoundland,** the act of kissing is called *whomping.*

In **Slovenia,** teenagers call kissing *zalizati,* or "to lick someone."

Alyson Noël

Tattooed Love Boys

"Can you even believe she's a virgin?" Janet whispered, twisting around in her seat, her lips pressed together in scorn, her clumpy, black lashes all waxy and spiky, like legs on a Halloween spider ring.

My eyes darted to the front of the room where Melody was reading from a play our English teacher had worked on all year. He dreamed of a fresh start on Broadway, a life free of bored and ungrateful students like us, and Melody, with her long, pale blond hair and tall lithe frame was a natural for the starring role.

She'd transferred to our suburban, middle-class school sometime during the last semester, and from the moment we laid eyes on her cork-heeled platforms, her tight Jordache jeans, and her little clutch purse crafted from the laminated cover of an old *Vogue* magazine, she was pretty much all we could talk about.

"She moved all the way from New York!" we'd whisper, gathered at our lunch table, hunched over mini doughnut six-packs and pink cans of Tab. "She's a model *and* an actress. I heard she even starred in a Jordache commercial! That's why she wears them all the time; she gets them for *free*!"

And even though we'd never speculated on the status of her virginity, we'd all heard about her boyfriend, a sophomore at the local high school, and so we drew our own conclusions.

But now, with Janet still looking at me, still smirking, I knew I'd just been handed some really great news. Because if someone as beautiful, cool, and exotic as Melody was still a virgin, then maybe there was hope for someone like me—a girl who'd never even been *kissed.*

I gazed at Janet, taking in her platinum-blond hair with the thick black line that ran straight down her part, the iridescent purple eye shadow that shimmered and flashed with each blink, and the darkly lined lips filled in with pink gloss, her face a perfectly detailed map of every *Glamour* magazine *don't,* that somehow, on her, managed to look so irresistibly lawless and right.

"Yup," she said, her eyes traveling over my favorite Ocean Pacific T-shirt, my tiny hoop earrings, and my wavy brown hair with the growing out "wings," until coming to rest on my new gold necklace with the small seashell charm. "Swear to God she's still a virgin. And. That's. Really. Bad."

I squirmed in my seat, crossing and uncrossing my legs, while thumping my pencil so hard it flew out of my hand and rolled off my desk. *Bad? Was she serious?* I mean, we were only in eighth grade! And even though I knew all about the small group of girls who were rumored to have "done it," up until that moment, I'd been sure they were a minority. But as I looked at Janet again, my palms grew wet and my face felt warm and flush, and I wondered what she'd say about me, if she ever learned of my status as the Ultimate Virgin.

But she just fished around in her brown suede bag, tossing a slightly squished cube of Bubble Yum onto my desk. And as my fingers peeled off the sticky wrapper, she leaned in even closer and said, "I swear she's gonna be *so* sorry if she doesn't get it over with soon. Older guys don't wait." She nodded, clearly an authority on the subject. "And I should know, my boyfriend graduated last year."

"From *high school*?" I said, my molars working overtime, furiously breaking down the huge wad of gum.

"Duh." She rolled her eyes. Then glancing quickly at Melody and back at me, she asked, "So what're you doing tomorrow?"

I thought of the new magenta dress I couldn't wait to wear, the ultra-high platforms I'd practiced walking in all week, and the sparkly pink lip gloss I'd been saving just for the occasion, and hoping to come off as cool, and funny, and maybe just the slightest bit jaded, I blew a small bubble, listened to its satisfying pop, and said, "Um, graduating eighth grade?" And then I laughed.

But she just shook her head, rolled her eyes, and said, "Whatever. Day after that."

And knowing better than to risk actually speaking again, I just shrugged.

"Good. Meet me at my house. We'll ride our bikes over to B&B and try on makeup." Then she turned back around in her seat, and ignored me for the rest of the day.

"You haven't even kissed a guy, have you?" she said, carefully coating my lips with a gloppy, fuchsia-colored gloss, squinting at my mouth as though she could tell just by looking.

"Of course I have," I said, my stomach beginning to twitch. Ever since I'd started hanging out with Janet, I suffered plenty of belly clenching, sweaty-palmed moments, but that didn't mean I was getting used to it.

She replaced the cap and stood back to survey her work. "You'll do better in high school." She nodded. "You act mature. Guys like that."

Janet had a habit of cataloging my more useful features, like a realtor pointing out appliances in a newly upgraded kitchen. Providing me with an entire list of supposed attributes, predicted to serve me well in the future.

"You have big boobs," she'd said one day as we sat across from each other in McDonald's, our straws scraping the bottom of our cups, searching for milk shake remains. "You should flaunt 'em more. Guys like that."

This was immediately followed by, "But don't ever cut your hair again. Guys think long hair is sexy."

Until Janet, I'd never thought of myself this way. Aside from a brief flirtation with Farrah Fawcett "wings," my hair had pretty much always been long, wavy, unchanged. And as for my "boobs," well, I'd successfully hid them since they first made an appearance back in fifth grade. It was only in junior high, when everyone else started to get them too, that I freed myself of ponchos and oversize sweaters. And as far as my perceived maturity went, well, that was really just the byproduct of my occasional, awkward bouts of shyness, which were either mistaken for wisdom or aloofness, depending on who was observing.

Then one day, we were lying by her pool, our bodies gleaming with baby oil, and surrounded by pieces of sun-reflecting foil, when she turned her head, opened one eye, squinted at me, and said, "So who's this guy you've supposedly kissed?"

I just lay there, solid, stiff, and silent. Her words echoing in my head, the conviction in her voice so clear and absolute.

I'd never been kissed.

And she knew it.

But then I shook my head, flipped the page on my magazine, and said, "Please. It's not like there's just one. I've kissed lots of guys."

"Yeah?" She sat up, eyeing me carefully. "Name one."

Realizing we'd gone to school with all the same people for the past two years, I had no choice but to invent someone. "You don't know him," I said, tossing my magazine aside and carefully placing my sunglasses on top. "He goes to another school."

"Which school?" she said, her face tight and pinched, not buying my act for a second.

I leaped off my lounge chair and headed for the edge of the pool. "It's in another county, another *state*," I said, and then I dove in, my arms and hands like arrows, aiming straight for the drain, hoping that by the time I resurfaced she'd have moved on to something else.

As obsessed as Janet was with the state of everyone's sex life, she remained incredibly hazy when it came to her own. And every time I tried to pin her down on just where this supposed, older, out-of-high-school-but-not-quite-in-college boyfriend actually was, she'd manage to steer the conversation right back to me. Having deemed me her summer project, making it her job to ensure I didn't start high school as "a loser who's never even been kissed."

And as pathetic as it was, I did nothing to stop her. Because even though I doubted most all of her stories, even though I knew her to be ninety-nine percent full of it, it's not like I was handling things so well on my own. And though I continued to roll my eyes and insist that I was *plenty experienced thank you very much,* privately I prayed she'd be able to save me.

I figured I'd blown my one and only chance back in seventh grade when I'd spent an entire week as the girlfriend of the cutest boy in my class. He'd asked me to "go" just before I climbed onto the bus, and under a fair amount of peer pressure from well-meaning friends, I agreed. The problem was, I didn't actually like him back. So after spending an entire week successfully avoiding him, I crammed a note into his locker suggesting we'd be better off "just friends."

I guess I didn't realize at the time how you don't have to actually *like* someone in order to kiss them. Though later I did learn that it really does help. And the only thing I managed to accomplish with that particular relationship was to make myself even less desirable, and ensure my neck as a hickey-free zone.

So reluctantly letting go of my dream of mutual love and longing, I quickly replaced it with one of glamour and excitement, the very two things my small town could never hope to deliver. But by the time I came under Janet's careful tutelage, I'd settled for just getting it over with.

So the day we begged her older brother to drop us off at the mall, Janet took one look around, nodded, and said, "Today's the day. Just look at that, would you?"

I followed the sweep of her hand, and as luck would have it, set up right there in the center of the mall was a giant skateboarding ramp. And lined up alongside it was an entire team of cute, messy-haired, adolescent skaters.

Janet's eyes moved among them as she elbowed me hard in the ribs. "You totally have to go for one of them. Any of them; it's not like it matters."

I shrugged, wiping my sweaty palms on the sides of my shorts and biting down on my lip, knowing that every single one of those guys was way out of my league. That any guy who made the circuit, doing mall expo skating for a large group of spectators, surely had a group of really hot girls to choose from. "I don't know," I said, gazing shyly at the one who was about to take to the ramp, the one with the dark tan, and brown, sun-streaked hair.

"Don't be ridiculous," she said, digging into her purse and handing me a piece of Bubble Yum. "Here, chew this so you won't have bad breath, and quit yanking your tube top up so high, I mean, *really*." She shook her head.

We stood there watching, our faces passive and bored, as Janet had cautioned against looking overly excited or impressed. And every time one of the skaters flipped a one-eighty before landing miraculously back on the ramp, Janet narrowed her eyes and gave me a quick, sharp nudge in the gut, a reminder that I dare not even think about clapping.

"This is perfect," she whispered, her blond hair swinging back and forth as she surveyed the crowd. "No competition *at all*. Seriously, we're the hottest ones here, check it out."

I glanced all around, seeing exhausted moms slumped over strollers, maxed-out dads trying to entertain their bored and crying sons, a group of middle-aged "mall walkers" taking a break between laps, and I knew she was right.

And sure enough, after about thirty minutes of ramp riding, the skaters took a break, and two of them headed straight for us.

I just stood there, scratching my arm and making sure to laugh in all the right moments as Janet made the usual small talk, somehow managing to flirt shamelessly while still remaining aloof, hard to get. And it wasn't long before one of them sidled up right beside me.

He wasn't the dark-haired one I'd hoped for. This guy's hair was dry, blond, and crispy, as though he washed it in salt water and never used conditioner, while his skin bore a deep, dark tan, a sharp contrast to the pale blue shade of his eyes, and as I focused in on his lips, I saw they were rough, chapped, and flaky.

It didn't matter that just ten seconds after he'd told me his name I'd already forgotten it. All that mattered was that he was absolutely perfect for what I was after, and that he seemed perfectly interested in participating. And as I gazed at him standing before me, taking in the dark blue markings of half a tattoo peeking out from under his sleeve, the baggy shorts that showcased his scar-covered knees, and the shoes that he'd personalized with drawings of lightning bolts and skulls, I could hardly believe my luck. I'd secretly clung to my dream of a glamorous, first kiss experience, and here I'd been presented with a Tattooed-Brand-Name-Sponsored-Semi-Pro-Skater. And in this mall, you just didn't get any more glamorous than that.

When their break was over, they returned to the ramp for more one-eighties, more tricks, and more applause from everyone but us, and the moment they finished, they were back by our sides, picking up where we left off.

"I have to go help break it down," no-name said, nodding at the ramp, while moving closer to me. "But can I get your number first?"

I shrugged, trying to act cool and nonchalant, just like Janet had coached me. "Do you have a pen?" I said, my hands fidgeting at my sides, fighting the urge to yank my tube top up higher.

He borrowed one from Janet since she always carried one in her purse (though she refused to bring along paper, insisting that if a guy really wanted your number then he had to be willing to meet you halfway), and we all stood there watching as he scribbled my number right onto his hand.

Then he moved in even closer and said, "Okay, so, I'll call you, okay?"

I nodded, every part of my body beginning to sweat, including my feet, watching as he closed his eyes and leaned toward me, happy to finally be getting this over with, happy that it was happening in front of Janet.

Two birds with one kiss.

At first his lips felt foreign, weird, scratchy. But it wasn't long before I adjusted, moved my gum to the side, and made room for his tongue.

At one point I opened my eye to peek first at him, then at Janet, who was busy making out with his friend, wondering just how long this was supposed to go on, not wanting to be the one to break it off first.

When I heard Janet laughing, I quickly pulled away and just stood there, my mouth feeling sloppy and wet, wondering if it would be rude to wipe it off right in front of him.

"Okay, well, later," they said, turning their backs and heading back to the ramp.

"Yeah, later," Janet called, grabbing my arm and leading me to the food court, wanting to celebrate the big moment with a visit to Hot Dog on a Stick.

Only I wasn't so eager to celebrate, because that would mean having to cop to it being my first time, and I definitely wasn't willing to do that.

"So? How was it?" she asked, eyeing me carefully, her face knowing and amused.

"Okay." I shrugged, hoping that was the appropriate answer. "I mean, it's not like I haven't done it before though."

She looked at me and narrowed her eyes, her brows merging together like two angry tadpoles. "Does it feel like your lips are still moving?" she asked.

"Totally!" I said, amazed that she knew.

But she just rolled her eyes as we got in line. "That's how it always feels the first time."

An Orange County native, **Alyson Noël** couldn't wait to get out of high school so she could flee suburbia and travel the world. And after several years of living in both Mykonos and Manhattan, she's amazed to find herself right back in The OC, writing about a time she hoped to never revisit—her adolescence.

The author of the teen novels *Faking 19, Art Geeks and Prom Queens, Laguna Cove, Kiss & Blog,* and *Saving Zoë,* as well as the adult novel *Fly Me to the Moon,* Alyson had successfully buried all memories of her very first kiss until asked to write this story. Now that Pandora's box has been opened, years of horrifying moments have resurfaced. She hopes to explore all of them in future novels. Visit her online at www.alysonnoel.com.

David Levithan
and
Nick Eliopulos

∽∘∾

A Brief History
of
First Kisses

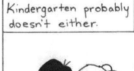

David Levithan's favorite song with the word "kiss" in the title is probably Louis Armstrong's "A Kiss to Build a Dream On," although the greatest, truest kissing moment in the music he listens to comes when Jeff Buckley sings "Kiss me out of desire, not consolation" in "Last Goodbye." David's books, most of which involve kissing of some sort, include *Boy Meets Boy, Wide Awake,* and *How They Met and Other Stories*. For more, stroll on by www.davidlevithan.com.

Nick Eliopulos enjoys both kissing and illustrating, but only one of these activities pays the bills. After a life-time of idle doodling, he published his first professional comic in 2007, in the anthology *Stuck in the Middle*. Nick grew up in Florida, lives in Manhattan, and routinely kiss-and-tells on his illustrated blog. You can read more at www.nickelio.com.

Scott Westerfeld

Braces

halfway to Bio
my tongue tip glides the metal
just behind your lips

Scott Westerfeld wrote
Uglies, Midnighters, and *Peeps*.
Haikus are quicker.

Donna Jo Napoli

So Many First Kisses

There's the one in fourth grade. Yup, fourth, I kid you not. Tommy, the son of a woman who worked for my grandfather. For some reason I cannot fathom now, we were supposed to kiss. And we did our part—obedient and dumb. Lips to lips. Once. Then I went inside and had diarrhea while my sister laughed.

Then there was Billy in sixth grade. Under a train trestle. Pretty much a repeat of fourth grade.

Were there others? I can't remember. And that's not just the effect of age. Fact: if there were kisses, they didn't count.

But Patrick in eighth grade, oh, Patrick, he counted.

Here's the scene.

Cheryl's having a party on her screened back porch. See the string of lights looping from the corners of the ceiling. The music is loud. Elvis Presley.

Wise men say only fools rush in

And there it goes. There what goes? My hormones, my blood, my heart. It takes only a moment, from one line to the next, and I am falling, I can't help falling, just as the music says. Can you hear it? No? Please go download it instantly. Listen.

That crazy artist who held his guitar across his knees and swiveled his hips and asked, so innocently, about the nature of sin—that's the man. He's doing it. Another in a tradition of dares. Do I eat a peach? Do I fall in love? Please, reader, try to feel it. Try to know the danger that excited every last one of us in that room. Be in that room.

Close your eyes and hear that mellow voice

crooning. Taste the onion dip—the real sour cream still coats your teeth. Smell Patrick's cologne. Canoe, you think. Or maybe English Leather.

Everything goes liquid. We're mostly water, after all. So we flow with the words, and everyone becomes a darling. Patrick is your darling. Red nose protruding above your head. Acne angry, always, but his eyes clear and happy. Sweat on his neck. New haircut, so short and clean. And your right hand inside his big left one, while your left sits on his shoulder and his right lightly touches the side of your waist. Feel that tentative hand.

Elvis won't let you not feel it. He speaks for you. He sings what is far too corny for you to ever say, but what you're so grateful he's making sound good, actually good, with that creamy, silky, velvety, honey, everything-good voice. Yes, the words are exactly what your heart means.

Oh, yes, let him take whatever he'll take. Please, God, if there is a god, please. And he does. He lets go of your hand and both of his meet at the small of your back and yours dare to circle his neck. So many dares tonight. You bury your head in the hollow of his throat and feel his Adam's apple go up in a gulp. And you keep dancing.

The essence of you flows, and it's true what the song says:

Some things are meant to be.

Something hot and wet touches your ear. Did he really lick it? Your legs shake. Your stomach lurches. This is literal—no metaphor, no cliché. You might be about to get sick. But you can't pull back. You're shameless now with the inevitability of it. You want him to "take your hand," like the song says, your hand and your whole life, oh, darling, take it all. And it's all right, this has to be all right, because that's what falling in love is: all right, nothing wrong.

You go home, cutting through Cheryl's backyard into your own. Everyone's asleep. You quietly get into your pajamas without even turning on the light. Then you climb into bed and stare through the black.

And a tap comes on the window. Well, no one taps your window. This is 1962, after all. Ordinary people don't tap windows in the middle of the night in 1962.

Another tap. You sit up straight. Are you losing your mind?

Another tap. You go to the window and open it. Patrick whispers, "Come out."

You go out in your pajamas. You sit beside him on the slab of cement that's supposed to be a porch. And he kisses you. Just a small, sweet kiss. Your hands take hold of the sides of his head and you're kissing him now, all over his cheeks and forehead and eyelids and nose and mouth. You can see yourself doing it, you know what's happening, but you can't stop yourself. You just kiss. And you're holding his ears so tight, maybe the poor boy is going deaf, but you keep kissing. Until you stop. And he stands up. From behind a bush he takes out a wooden paddle. It's from the club he's in. He says, "Keep it for me, would you?" It means you're his girl. You can't believe it. You're not in his crowd. You're not one of the popular kids. But his paddle is in your hands. He leaves and you go inside.

You can't fall asleep. The paddle is shellac slick.

Maybe an hour later, there's another tap at the window. You rush to open it. "I need it back." "The paddle?" "Yes." You hand it out through the window. He doesn't offer an explanation. You don't ask.

Only fools rush in. Elvis warned you, even as he primed you. The motor had to start, no matter that no one was in the driver's seat. It was meant to be. You close your eyes and sleep like the dead.

Forty years later, Patrick writes you an e-mail. You start a mundane exchange. Then you ask him about that night. And he doesn't remember it. He says you must have made it up. He's never kissed you. He always wanted to, always wondered who would be the first to really kiss you.

Donna Jo Napoll did not grow up wanting to be a writer She loved books and she loved writing, but she loved just about everything else, too. School was a haven, particularly school libraries. It was after a personal tragedy that she came to writing, almost as a kind of whacked-out therapy. It worked; she got over her grief. But she didn't get over writing. She has five children, one grandson, and a cat. She teaches linguistics, gardens, dances, does yoga, bakes bread, pots, and draws. She has about sixty fiction books in print.

The Top Ten Worst
Pre-Kiss Foods

10. Sushi

9. Hot peppers

8. Everything bagels

7. Cheese

6. Pickles

5. Beans

4. Spinach or other green, leafy vegetables

3. Doritos

2. Soda

And the #1 Worst Pre-Kiss Food is a two-way tie:

 Garlic & Onions

Lauren Myracle

Lips, Tongues, and Dr Pepper

Just so you know: this story does not have a happy ending (other than the fact that it *does* eventually end). Life goes on, what doesn't kill you makes you stronger, blah blah blah. There is very little chance I will ever see Mickey O'Reilly again. This is what I need to remember.

But I'm a great believer in belching out the embarrassment of our lives for the benefit of others, as in, *"She did what?" "Oh . . . the horror."* *At least I've managed to navigate the world better than she did, poor dear.*

So here goes:

I met Mickey at debate camp. This is embarrassing detail number one, because seriously, who goes to debate camp? Leslie Cardoza, who had highlights and honeydews and overall hotness . . . well, guess what? Didn't go to debate camp. The bus transporting Leslie to baton-twirling camp just kept chugging along as my debate camp bus exited the interstate. I waved, but Leslie didn't wave back.

Embarrassing detail number two: I was fifteen years old. I was fifteen, and I had yet to kiss a boy. I'd read about kissing, and I'd seen plenty of kissing on TV and at the movies, and I'd listened in awe as my best friend, Kristin, shared the details of her many kissing adventures. But somehow, all of that kissing had just . . . passed me by.

And here's embarrassing detail number three: while I really wanted to be kissed, I was terrified of the actual moment. Terrified! Because a fifteen-year-old should know what do to when a cute guy's lips come closer and closer, shouldn't she? A fifteen-year-old should yearn to meet those lips with her own, to make smoochy sounds, to take little nippy lip bites, and eventually—because it has to happen, it's inevitable—a fifteen-year-old should want to part her lips and go for the tongue.

But let's take a moment to debate the merits of this proposition, shall we?

The tongue is a muscle. The tongue is a squirmy hunk of flesh that's pink and slick, and underneath are cordy veins.

It is not a rose.

It is not a raspberry-infused chocolate.

Why would *anyone* want to part her lips and go for the tongue?

Yet people kiss each other all the time, and common wisdom touts the experience as "natural." That you'll "know what to do" when the time comes. That if you simply relax into the moment, the moment will take care of itself. You'll be transported.

Er . . . yeah.

Plenty of girls, I'm sure, have stood with their

backs pressed against trees on a sultry summer evening, their heads swirling with phrases like "constitutional amendment" and "it is self-evident" and "Judge, move to strike!" Their hearts have raced beneath thin cotton T-shirts. They've sensed the slow lean in as Mickey's dark eyes locked on theirs, and they've indubitably responded with a lean in of their own.

Although, egads. How many debate girls did Mickey in fact kiss? And who knows, maybe he kissed other girls, too. Non-debate girls. *Perhaps even baton-twirling girls.* Is that Leslie Cardoza I spot, giggling and tugging Mickey closer? That wench!

Except, come on. Baton-twirling camp was a hundred miles up the highway.

Oh. My. God. How did Leslie slink into Mickey's embrace from a hundred miles up the highway? Did she have a teleportation device? Was she wearing her white calfskin booties with tassels? Double wench!

Whoa. Stop. Do you see what happens when

you live to the ripe age of fifteen before experiencing your first kiss? Your brain doesn't want to go back to the moment of trauma. It just doesn't want to go there. And when it does, it gets things wrong *on purpose*. It says, "Ooh, let's bad-mouth Leslie Cardoza instead! That'll be way more fun than remembering what a poor, dumb pudding you were!"

LESLIE CARDOZA IS NOT A WENCH. (Anymore.) (I don't think.) (Although she did wear those white calfskin booties with infuriating regularity, and not just on game days.)

Forget Leslie Cardoza.

I'm fifteen, I'm at debate camp, and my back is pressed against a massive oak as Mickey weaves his fingers through mine. Other debate camp lovers murmur and giggle from their spots on the campus quad; almost every tree is taken. Kristin has coupled for the summer with Brad, a broad and goofy Midwesterner who says "za" instead of "pizza," and I can hear them nuzzling two oaks over. Mickey is cuter than Brad, with his dark eyes and wavy blond hair, but Brad is funnier. Brad makes Kristin laugh.

Mickey leans in toward me, and I think I might faint. It's the tongue thing, for starters, but also because I really really *really* need to pee. If only I hadn't swigged down that third Dr Pepper in the campus cafeteria, land of free refills! Or, option number two: if only I'd made a pit stop at the girl's room as Mickey and I strolled outside after dinner! But girls aren't supposed to pee, just as they aren't supposed to sweat or fart. Or—cue ominous music—do anything else involving bodily expulsions.

"Will you quit it?" Mickey asks, to stop me from fidgeting. Mickey puts his hands on my shoulders, but he isn't being macho or obnoxious. He's jittery, too, I think. I'm so nervous that I'm making *him* nervous. We have absolutely nothing in common—I'm a Southern prep school girl, he's from a working-class family in the Bronx—and our relationship is based on little more than a smile shared on the first day of camp. We're like two tadpoles fluttering and bumping in a pond. We don't even *know* how to know each other, not in any real way.

Mickey holds me still, and it's surprisingly nice, despite the nerves and the caffeine and the hyperawareness of how strange it is to be in a field populated entirely by debate kids making out.

But then.

Oh, this is painful.

You know what's coming, don't you?

Mickey's lips touch mine, and it stirs something deep within me, something carbonated and syrupy sweet. To this day I don't know why Dr Pepper is called "Dr Pepper"—I understand neither the "doctor" nor the "pepper"—but I do know it tastes a heck of a lot better going down than coming up. Also, on the whole romance meter thing? It is really, really gross to burp into your boyfriend's mouth. This is simply not a point to be argued.

Oh, poo.

If only I'd twirled the baton.

Lauren Myracle is the author of many books for tweens and teens, including the *New York Times* bestsellers *ttyl*; *ttfn*; *l8r, g8r*; and *Twelve*. Readers have called Lauren's books "hilarious," "the best ever," and "so good I couldn't stop to go to the bathroom." Lauren is most pleased, however, by the fan who wrote, "I can't believe they were written by a—cough, cough—grown-up!" She likes both kissing and Dr Pepper very much . . . though preferably not combined.

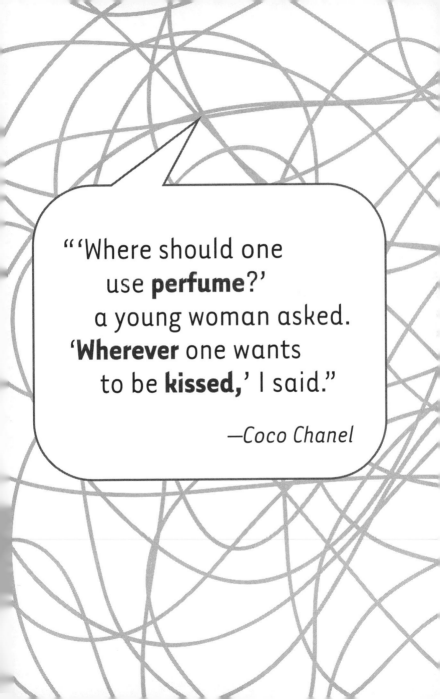

"'Where should one use **perfume**?' a young woman asked. '**Wherever** one wants to be **kissed,**' I said."

—*Coco Chanel*

About the Editor

Cylin Busby claims that she had her first kiss at age fourteen (but in reality, it was dangerously close to her fifteenth birthday). She is a former children's book editor and the author of several fiction and nonfiction books for young readers, including the Date Him or Dump Him? series. She lives in Los Angeles with her husband and son and you can visit her on the Web at www.cylinbusby.com.